Praise for *Oh*

"Wow, what a memoir! It's so raw and good and important. The first step in healing is radical honesty. Frazier's memoir is as honest and healing as they come."

— Jedidiah Jenkins, *New York Times* best-selling author of *To Shake the Sleeping Self* and *Like Streams to the Ocean*

"Phew. I found myself consumed while reading this stunning memoir. In it, Lindsey beautifully captures what it means to be wholly human. No fairy-tale beginnings or endings. Just a whole lot of discomfort, perseverance, growth, and joy. Lindsey is a damn good human, and this is a damn good book. Read it immediately, friend. You'll be glad you did."

— Nick Laparra, host of the *Let's Give A Damn* podcast, environmentalist, speaker, and investigative journalist

"A stunning account of life's twists and turns, *Oh Love, Come Close* is impossible to put down and will keep you locked in from start to finish. Frazier's memoir is not only one of the most honest and raw books I've read in some time, it is downright inspiring. If only we were all so bold to go back and examine our stories so closely, the world would be a much richer place."

— Leslie Jordan, Grammy-nominated singer-songwriter and executive director of The Fold

OH LOVE, COME CLOSE

OH LOVE, COME CLOSE

A MEMOIR

LINDSEY FRAZIER

DEXTERITY
NASHVILLE

604 Magnolia Lane
Nashville, TN 37211

Some names and identifying details have been changed to protect the privacy of individuals.

Printed in the United States of America

First edition: 2023
10 9 8 7 6 5 4 3 2 1

ISBN: 978-1-947297-58-6 (Paperback)
ISBN: 978-1-947297-59-3 (E-book)

Publisher's Cataloging-in-Publication Data

Names: Frazier, Lindsey E., author.
Title: Oh love , come close : a memoir / Lindsey Frazier.
Description: Nashville, TN: Dexterity, 2022.
Identifiers: ISBN: 978-1-947297-58-6 (paperback) | 978-1-947297-59-3 (ebook)
Subjects: LCSH Frazier, Lindsey E. | Women--Biography. | Authors, American--21st century—Biography. | Nashville (Tenn.)--Biography. | Marriage. | Bisexual women--United States--Biography. | Self-actualization (Psychology). | Christian biography. | BISAC BIOGRAPHY & AUTOBIOGRAPHY / Personal Memoirs | FAMILY & RELATIONSHIPS / Marriage & Long-Term Relationships | BODY, MIND & SPIRIT / Healing / General Classification: LCC PS3606.R4285 2022 | DDC 818/.603—dc23

Cover design by Zoe Norvell
Interior design by Mallory Collins

To you who, like me, have known feeling hidden and lonely.
My words are for us. You're not alone.

To the ones I've hurt along the way, I'm sorry.
You deserved better.

To little Lindsey, you aren't broken.
To be vulnerable is to be brave, and you are
the bravest. It's safe to cry again.

Did you know
The songbird only sings
To find her love
And defend her young?

In those early twilight hours
As the sky shifts
From gray to bright blue
Her song is the sound
Of pursuit and protection
Of longing and loyalty

Have you heard it?
Do you hear it now?

Deep within us is the love
We lost to winter
Where the ground grew
Hard and cold
Where the sun stayed
hidden longer

If we wait patiently
And begin to listen
That song will rise up
In perfect time
Its melody familiar
Giving us the courage

To sing and keep singing

—Leslie Jordan

Contents

one

The End

"I want a divorce."

We'd been married only a week. Still, the words rolled off my tongue like I'd been practicing them.

I slipped the diamond off my finger and threw it across the room at him. He flinched as it ricocheted off the wall and landed next to the couch.

We were told by those who knew us not to get married. *You're not ready*, they'd said. *She's not good for you. Whenever she's around, there's drama.* They felt the heat of our explosions, but this was our own fault. We could never hide our fights well. Maybe we should have listened.

My stomach tightened at the sight of his sudden despair. The atmosphere had turned quiet, and maybe that was the whole point of me throwing the ring: to stop the screaming. He looked up from the floor and caught my eyes with his. Both of us at a loss for words, though it was possible we'd been thinking the same thing: *What are we supposed to do now?*

My rage subsided, and with no anger left to hide behind, I felt vulnerable. My eyes burned as I held back a flood of tears. I was aware that I had just ripped his heart right out of his chest, watching the weight of grief take hold of the man I'd vowed to love.

My own empathy toward my husband caught me by surprise. Empathy meant considering the pain of someone else, which was an unnatural feeling for me. It wasn't that I didn't care about other people or feel sad when someone I loved was in pain, but the culture I was raised in taught me that being sad never solved any problems. Growing up, there hadn't been much time for softness.

I never wanted to hurt Jonathan. All I ever wanted was for our relationship to be easier than it was—for the years of relational baggage in my story to stay hidden, to not affect my life in the present day. What I wanted was to naturally find all I needed in a marriage with him, having believed that once we got married, everything would be okay. However, what I found out, rather quickly, was that though I might be able to run far from the truth, I could never outrun the heart that beats life into me every day. I never wanted to run from my marriage either; I only ever wanted to find myself *in* him. To truly become one. To lie with him, cuddle with him, and kiss him. But there was too much pain in the way.

I could feel the spinning come on like a tornado: His tears. My shame. His confusion. My frantic search for a solution.

I began to pace the room. *I have to fix this.* He sat down. *I need to tell him.*

I joined him on the floor. I knew this would not be easy—but I would not sugarcoat it. He needed to know the truth.

"I'm so sorry I've done this to you." His arms lay helpless in his lap, with no strength left in them. I picked up his hands and gently held them in mine. My own humiliation had started to kick in. I let the tears fall, mirroring the emotion I saw in his eyes. "But I don't think I can do this anymore."

I paused. He was motionless. Not even a flinch. Maybe he was too tired, or maybe the shock of hearing I was giving up already was a little too much to bear.

"Jonathan, I think I'm gay."

He furrowed his brow, and I could tell he was processing. I felt exposed as his eyes still held mine. I squeezed his hands a little to cue that it was his turn to speak . . . if he had anything left to say. But he didn't utter a single word. I was expecting confusion, maybe even anger. But I wasn't expecting *nothing.*

I've broken him, I thought. *Oh God, I'm sorry we didn't listen.*

He let go of my hands and stood. He walked into the kitchen, and I tried hard to be still. Watching him, waiting for the moment he would blow up. *I've never seen him blow up before.* I prepared myself for the worst. *Does he have it in him?* He moved past the block of knives, past the sink, and reached for the paper towels. He ripped one off and blew his nose. I relaxed, noticing how tense my body had become. He threw the paper towel away and grabbed another one before walking back over to me. Then he sat back down in front of me and took my hands back in his. I felt helpless to the softness of his touch. *He deserves someone better.* My eyes lowered at the insistence of my own shame.

"Lindsey," he pleaded, "please, will you go talk to someone?" I sensed from the ache of his voice that he felt the same emptiness I did. I thought this part of me, the part where I suffered with desire to be loved and held by another woman, would fade away after marrying him. But I was wrong. Our marriage only amplified the loss I felt. This was not the only problem my marriage faced. It was just the easiest one to name.

"I am lost, Jonathan." He squeezed my hands tighter before he let go. Something in his grip told me he already knew—as if he had seen right through me all this time—and he wasn't leaving, not yet, not this soon. I wiped my tears and stood up to grab my things.

"Where are you going?" he asked, concerned.

I walked to the coat closet and reached for my jacket. "I'm going to find help!" Just like he had asked. He may not have meant "right this moment," but I didn't want to wait. What was sulking about it going to do? I threw the coat around my shoulders, slid my arms in, and raised my hood before stepping outside. I would go searching for the answer; someone had to have it.

"I'll be home soon." By promising my return, I was putting to rest any fear of a suicide attempt. He'd experienced my ideation before, and it scared him.

I shut the door behind me and tried to dodge the freezing rain as I ran to my car. No matter how fast I ran, though, I could not escape the cold water pelting my face. By the time I reached the car, my coat was soaked and so were my shoes—the perks of living in an apartment with a parking lot instead of a driveaway. I climbed into the driver's seat and quickly threw the wet coat over to the passenger's side. I turned the dial for the heat all the way up—something that would bug Jonathan. When I was hot, like any normal person, I turned the dial to the coolest setting of AC possible, and I turned it toward the hottest setting when cold. He wondered why I was so extreme, why I didn't just move it a little right or left of the center and wait patiently for the car to adjust to a temperature of my approval. I'd state my answer, as if it was extremely simple: "Why be patient when we can speed up the process?"

I rubbed my arms and legs to keep warm, waiting until the heat filled the car. I left the music off. I found comfort in the strangely quiet space after such a loud argument. I was finally alone, and the facade could come off.

I placed my head in my hands and let myself cry for a moment before driving off.

No clear answer presented itself the day I left my apartment, vowing to return with one. Two years went by, and the effects of a struggling marriage began to take their toll on us. I had to imagine that everyone around us felt it too, based on the tone of the room whenever we entered it. Our community was just as tired as we were from carrying lifeless legs to a finish line none of us could see ahead. Even still, they held onto hope.

It was a warm summer evening, and I was outside kicking rocks underneath my feet, enjoying a moment alone. Everyone was inside now, probably crowded around dinner tables or maybe tucking their little ones into bed. Wherever the people were, they were not next to me, and for just a moment, gravity lifted its weight off my chest. Aloneness meant I was free of expectations, free from facing the bitter reminder of my inability to love my husband every time he asked me to come close to him. *I am alone, and I am at peace.*

My phone rang. I pulled it from my pocket and noticed it was not a number I was familiar with. A call from an unidentified number was nothing unusual, except that instead of letting it go to voicemail, I was inclined to answer it.

Then I heard her voice. It was strong and stable. Could it be that she possessed something I didn't? A hope that was not yet weary?

The wind brushed against my face as the clouds moved across the setting sun.

Something was coming. I sensed it in the stillness.

two

Somewhere, Together

I eyed the premade margarita mix and poured a little extra tequila into my cup. I was not someone who abused alcohol regularly, but I was beginning to question my intake as my tolerance level elevated. I didn't want to get drunk, but I could use an extra hand in taking the edge off the daily anxiety I felt.

I took a big sip and watched my daughter in the next room, standing on her toes and wobbling confidently around the furniture, holding onto anything she could reach for some solidity. She was just learning to take her first steps, and I admired her courage to keep trying after so many falls.

Her tiny fingers gripped the edge of the couch as she reached her toes out in front of her. *Well, she knows where she wants to go*, I thought. Something I struggled to know for myself. My daughter was a strong-willed child, so I knew wherever she was set on arriving, she'd get there. She was stubborn, like me. I watched her loosen her grip.

One step.

Two steps.

A fall.

Her dad and I cheered and clapped for her anyway. I was already walking toward her when she reached out her arms and I met her with mine. I kept the tone of my voice enthusiastic as I picked her up and kissed her cheek. It wasn't one minute before she wiggled out of my arms to try walking again. I set her on her feet and gave her my hand. I knew that soon she wouldn't need me for stability; she'd find her own balance.

Watching her tiptoe across the floor settled the chaos in my heart. She was my peace—a deep well of cold, satisfying water after two years of agonizing thirst. She was someone my husband and I created, together. A reminder that not everything we shared was dead.

Her adoration for the two of us tightened the strings of a love torn and frayed. We knew—if nothing else—a family intact, for her, was worth preserving. But how long could he and I do this? Neither of us knew.

I removed my hand from her fingers and let her take only one finger of mine to balance with. She was getting it. It was hard not to smile when I looked at her. The joy on her face was contagious.

I motioned for her dad to trade places with me so I could get some fresh air. He came over, and I left my drink on the counter before I walked outside.

Back and forth, I paced the driveway, thinking about the conversation I'd had with the woman on the phone—the proposition she had made to meet weekly. I was intrigued by her confidence, that we'd get to where we wanted to go. I needed a guide, or maybe just a friend—someone who would not let go of my hand when I wanted to run back toward the depression I was growing comfortable living in. I had just accepted the loss I felt daily because it felt inevitable.

I lifted my eyes up to the sky.

Will the clouds part today? I wondered.

Thick, gray clouds moved in spontaneity, flirting with the sun like a girl playfully swishing her dress right to left, hoping to get her subject's attention. I was taken by the dance.

The sun pushed her way through as the clouds parted in reverence. I raised my arm to shelter my eyes. It was all so bright, but I welcomed the warmth on my face. I closed my eyes and sat down on the gravel driveway. The rocks beneath me reminded me of days I used to walk barefoot to the lake when I was a young girl. I was always too eager to grab my sandals before running to the boat. Having cut my foot on a stone once, I knew how to toe the rock before applying all my weight into a full step. If you could find the smooth spots, walking on rocks was as gentle as walking on sand. But when you weren't careful, one wrong step felt like a blade into the arch of your foot. Sometimes, when my grandmother would catch me before I ran off, she'd holler, "Where are your shoes?"

And I'd holler back, already breezing by, "I don't need them, Mimi! I'm being careful!" I'd like to think I'm still careful today. Though I am stubborn, I've learned some lessons along the way. Too many paths I thought were smooth left my feet a bloody mess.

The heat on my face reminded me of boat days. The days when there was no need for schedules or answers, only an agenda to find heaven in the water. The lake gave me the most tangible example of a refuge.

If I could just go back there.

The woman I'd spoken to on the phone was confident that we'd get *somewhere,* together.

"I believe I can help you," she'd said. But how could she be so certain? She'd suggested we meet twice a week, for two hours each day. She had put a plan in place, but I was still wondering if this would all be a waste of our time. "Are you feeling good about this?" she'd asked me, referring to her plan.

There was no need to hide my weariness from her. She was a therapist. Her role was to help carry the burden of the broken on their long walk home.

"I'm up for trying," I'd told her.

I wanted to trust her optimism, but I'd sat in front of a different therapist before. After telling her I was gay, she'd said, "I don't think I can help you. I need to refer you to someone else." We had cut our time short, but not before I had relaxed the arm holding her at a distance. I walked out of her office that day very aware that I was a problem no one knew how to fix.

Jen, the woman I had spoken to on the phone, was a practical thinker who made plans and set dates. She was encouraging in our brief conversation, but none of her words comforted quite like the words she never actually said. Her language implied, *I'm here now. You are not alone.*

three

Where It Begins

Fall rushed in with its heroic nature: cooler temps and a summons to get lost in the trails of a neighboring state park. A chilly hike felt like a friendly invitation to a change of scenery after a stifling hot Southern summer.

I was driving to Jen's house for the first time, where she and I would meet weekly. The drive was ten miles of breathtaking beauty through the charming hills of Tennessee. I inhaled the fresh air as I rolled my window down. As I breathed in deep, I reminded myself how good it felt to be alive. I made the final turn onto a cul-de-sac and stopped in front of a large redbrick home.

This is where she lives? I laughed sarcastically. *In a mansion?* What I had come to experience from living in the South was that wealthy women carried themselves a bit . . . presumptuously. One could usually pinpoint a woman's tax bracket by the rock on her finger, her perfectly blown-out hair, and yoga pants that cost more than one should pay for pants to sweat in. But that was not how Jen had carried herself the day I first met her. She and I had met for a quick coffee after our first phone call. My first impression of her, her gray Chuck Taylors and loose, V-neck T-shirt made me feel at ease, like she'd leveled the playing field between us. In reality, it was the kindness she carried that made me feel so welcome—but it helped to know that she and I had similar taste in style. So, I guess, in a way, it was my own fault for stereotyping and being so shocked by her enormous house.

I put the car in park and turned off the engine before I reached into the back seat and unlatched my daughter's seat belt. It was October, and she had just had her first birthday. She didn't know it then, but I knew the best present I could give her was stepping into this mansion for the very first time. I opened her door and watched as she stretched her arms out toward me. I pulled her up onto my hip, giving her a kiss on her head before I shut the car door behind us.

The wind blew through the trees, loosening the autumn leaves from the branches that held them, creating a few beams of sunlight on the sidewalk as we walked up to Jen's house.

I can see the sun is still pushing her way through the clouds.
Giving us her light, her nurturing presence.
Knowing when we need her most.
She'd move earth and sky to get to us.
I love her strong will.

I took a deep breath. "It's gonna be fine," I assured my daughter, but I knew it was not really her I was trying to convince.

Before I could knock, the door swung open. Jen was energetic upon our arrival. I was feeling excited too, but I struggled to match her intensity; I knew the work ahead of me. I forced a smile anyway. She hugged me as we walked inside. Her care eased some of my anxiety.

I watched my daughter respond openly to Jen's playfulness toward her. She liked her already, which was a great thing considering I would be spending so much time with her. I was hoping not to bring my baby to every session, though, considering the setup wasn't ideal. Also, how nice it was to have a few hours alone.

Jen's home was welcoming and cozy; a lit candle filled the entryway with the comforting scent of vanilla and cinnamon sticks. The rooms were spacious, with tall ceilings and dark cherry-stained hardwood floors. Large windows lined the living room, giving me a preview of a wooded backyard. *It feels good in here*, I thought.

She led me to a room with french doors. This was where we'd be meeting.

I caught my reflection in a mirror that hung outside the room. I saw a woman, tattered. Lost. A woman whose eyes failed miserably at covering up the despair she felt in her own heart. I offered myself a smile. Not all hope was lost—not just yet.

This was my last effort to find that lost woman, to bring her home. If this failed, I'd choose to leave my husband—or rather, cut him loose. He deserved a better wife; I knew that much. The guilt of my narrative haunted me: *You'll never love him the way he needs to be loved. You're not good enough.*

"I'm so glad you're here," Jen said, interrupting my thoughts.

I stepped through the french doors and sat down on a love seat just a few feet across from her.

"Are you ready to get started?" I was relieved to see more windows just behind her. A comfort, knowing that whenever this room became stifling hot and oxygen grew hard to come by, I could step outside and feel my lungs expand. For now, I was doing okay. *I am still breathing.*

Jen introduced herself formally, giving me background information and the credentials she'd earned to become a licensed therapist. Really, though, she was just offering me a few more minutes to settle in before my turn to talk. *Where do I even start?* I couldn't afford to understate the pain I'd been feeling. There was too much at stake.

Jen didn't seem to care for pretending anyway. She seemed far less concerned about my approval than she did about me becoming free. She didn't strike me as one for cheap talk.

"So, tell me, Lindsey." My mind focused on her words. "Why are you here today?"

So, this is where it all begins.

"I don't really know where to start . . ." I paused. She was letting me work out my thoughts. "I am at the end of myself. I guess I'm just hoping you can help me." I stated it as plainly as I could. "I just can't do this alone."

She spoke kindly: "Can you tell me a little more about what's causing you so much pain?"

I started thinking about the list: the one I'd written down just days earlier, full of things I hated about myself, things that had happened to me, things I chose. I wrote down everything that held me back from receiving the persistent love of a partner who could have left me long ago. I made a list because I had to get it on paper—all the things I wanted to be healed from. *I'm here because of that list.* I envisioned the piece of white scrap paper, every line filled in with black ink, impossible to erase.

Thinking about the "things," or issues, or whatever you want to call them, overwhelmed me. "Just fix the things on the list!" I wanted to plead with Jen. The sheet of paper looked more like a checklist at a doctor's office. I thought back on my last medical visit, when the nurses handed me a sheet of paper with an outline of a human body on it. "Circle the part of the body that hurts," the directions said.

Can I just circle the whole body?

My mind was restless. My heart felt broken, but I was the one who'd caused the brokenness. "Just give me a new heart," I wanted to say.

Jen's voice broke through my downward spiral, for I had only *thought* about answering her. I hadn't actually answered her yet. "You're not from Tennessee, right? What brought you here?"

A simpler question. I repositioned myself on the love seat and cleared my throat. This was easier to tackle. I'd memorized every detail. I looked at my daughter down on the floor beside me, content playing with the toys I had brought for her. *Should I cover her ears? Will this story scare her?*

I took a deep breath. "I moved here in 2006. I was afraid to stay living where I was." I stopped to swallow the excess saliva that had gathered at the back of my throat. "My friend was raped and murdered that March. So, I moved away in July."

Keep going, I encouraged myself.

"After the man raped her, he slit her throat and left her to die, naked, in the shower. He ransacked her home and set it on fire."

The word *ransacked* pulled me back to the present moment. It was a funny word to me, one I had never used before I read it in the newspaper after my friend's death. Now, when I described her murder, I used it all the time—like I was re-reading the details of her gruesome death straight from the Monday morning news.

The pain of the story wasn't fresh anymore; now it was comprised of facts. Facts I replayed over and over as I imagined myself in the same scenario with every strange sound I heard in the middle of the night, every moment I walked alone to my car, every time I saw a strange man look my body up and down like he was planning an exotic, sexual experience with me. I stored the facts in my head and tried hard to separate them from my heart. But the truth was, they *lived* in my heart. .

As Jen waited for me to finish the story, I got lost in my thoughts. I realized that maybe the moment I disconnected from the gory details, when my heart could no longer handle the emotions of such a devastating truth, was the day I saw his face in court. Right there, sitting five rows in front of me, was the man who'd raped my friend before slitting her throat—his hands and feet bound and head freshly shaven. He had only a number for an identity now, but to me, he still had a name. And though I didn't know him, I would never forget that name.

Maybe my heart broke when my slain friend's grieving mother, incapable of restraining her pain, took the stand. Her only daughter, gone. She looked at the numbered identity and told him to rot in hell.

Or maybe my heart broke for the last time because of my own shame for considering the tears of the tightly bound man who broke down in sobs, knowing his fate was irreversible, as he turned toward her family to plead for their forgiveness.

No, no. They're not ready for forgiveness.

"I don't feel the sadness anymore." I escaped from the memory and looked at Jen. "I quit feeling sad a long time ago.

"Lynsey was her name. She and I shared it. Feels like the only tie I have left to her."

Jen was attentive, showing me she could handle such a heartbreaking story. My daughter was in her own world, undisturbed by the details of a heinous murder story.

"The thing is, Lynsey's dad was a fireman. His station was the one called when a neighbor saw smoke rising from the home. But when they showed up, they wouldn't let him go inside. He knew his daughter was in there . . ." I drew a long breath. "She died from a loss of blood."

I read the look of concern on Jen's face. The story felt uniquely shocking because the detail was so unbelievable, making it feel like fiction. Yet nothing was fictional about this. It was real, and it devastated an entire town.

"I am so sorry," she offered, just like so many others had

after they heard the story. But I was tired of sorrys. I shrugged my shoulders in apathy. There was nothing a sorry could fix, change, or heal.

I found out quickly, living in the South and close to the campus of a private Christian college, that these types of stories didn't go over well at weekend house parties. Whenever anyone realized I didn't attend one of the local colleges and wasn't pursuing any sort of music career, they'd curiously ask why I moved to Nashville. So, I told them in the most basic, honest way: "My friend was murdered, so I just needed to leave town." They'd shift awkwardly, offering very unprepared-for sympathetic condolences. They meant well. We moved on. "Well, it was nice to meet you!"

Okay, so maybe a first-time introduction wasn't the right time for me to give them this information, though is there ever a good time to talk about a friend's murder? Maybe, for the first time, the religious South was starting to learn that you can't actually "bless your heart" out of a brutal murder story.

The next time I met someone new, wanting to avoid the awkward tension, I adjusted to a little more culturally acceptable answer: "Oh, I just needed a change of scenery!" I'd give a kind smile and pretend there was nothing more to it. Though, in the end, I wonder if that response was a way of blessing my own weary heart.

"I was scared to stay in the town I grew up in," I told Jen, "so I packed my bags and told my parents I was moving to Nashville."

I'd given her so much already, but Jen sat there as if we

still had more to talk about. And there *was* more. I was only getting started.

"Do you really want all the details of my friend's death?" I asked her.

"Do you feel a need to protect me, Lindsey?"

Maybe I did. Or rather, I felt a need to protect myself from reliving it. I sank deeper into the couch. I was here to talk about *everything*. I was getting ready to tell her the story—my story. For the first time in a long time, I'd start from the very beginning.

four

Something Tragic

The last bell rang, and I hurried to my seat. "Hey, Linds," she whispered, smiling at me with her beautiful, contagious smile.

It was fifth period, history class. If any class reminded me just how long a minute really is, it was history. The afternoon sunshine heated the room, making our already exhausted minds susceptible to shutting down in a hypnotic daze. I was painfully aware of how stuck I was inside history class, not outside running around in one of the first perfect days of an Indiana spring.

Today we were discussing debate. Desks facing inward bordered two walls of the classroom, leaving a large walking space in the middle of the room for our teacher to roam and mediate. He thought it was important for us to understand that healthy debates and healthy conflicts call for eye contact. If we were to disagree on something, at least we'd have to face each other on it. In a school known for cliques, fights, and hair left on the floor after a lunchroom brawl, we all could learn a lesson in healthy disagreements. We only had forty-five minutes, so we started right in.

First topic: Who agrees that the legal age for buying cigarettes should be eighteen? Who disagrees? Why? *Easy*, I thought. *The legal age should be sixteen, when you can drive.* Most of the class had something to say about this. Probably because a lot of teens smoked. I couldn't have cared less though. Although I smoked occasionally, I didn't like the aftertaste of cigarettes.

Second topic: Who agrees that abortion should be a legal right for all women? Who disagrees? Why? I didn't have an easy answer for this. I sat silently and observed the conversations around me. I didn't know if I agreed or disagreed. One classmate spoke up, arguing that abortion should "absolutely be illegal" and leaving no room for discussion. But that's not how an actual debate works, so someone else piped up.

"But what if a girl was raped?"

That seemed to hit a collective nerve. Our teacher stepped back, allowing us to enter the conflict, only interjecting to turn the conversation back to abortion instead of the rabbit trail of what qualifies as consensual or nonconsensual sex. The classroom was loud with opinions.

The debate was abruptly cut short at the sound of Lynsey pushing herself out of her desk, visibly upset, then bolting out of the room. I looked to the only adult, and he nodded for me to follow her.

I walked into the hallway and looked around. I could not see her, but she couldn't have gone far. She must have been running.

The closest place to hide was the girls' restroom just a few doors down from ours. I opened the door and called her name softly. I couldn't tell if she was in there. It looked completely empty. As I turned to leave and check another spot, I heard a few sniffs in the back stall. I moved inside and let the door close behind me.

"Hey, Lynz, it's me," I said gently. She stepped out of the stall, and a sunbeam from the window above her caught the top of her head. She wiped the makeup from her eyes. I knew why she was crying.

When we were in the eighth grade, Lynsey's best friend, Jessica, was murdered in her home. The story was all over the news after it happened. A young girl, thirteen years old, was beaten to death with a hammer after being raped by a boy who'd snuck into her home in the middle of the night. He was her next-door neighbor. When he pled not guilty, it forced a full investigative trial—featuring horrifying images no child should witness, especially of their dead best friend. I knew the details because when you get a bunch of eighth graders in a courtroom for a murder investigation, they will talk about those details for years to come.

I went to Jessica's viewing, which was the day before the funeral. I walked to the open casket, and her face looked nothing like the 8 × 10 photo sitting upright next to her body. The sight shocked me. I still remember the sounds of grief throughout the funeral home. It was not a quiet room.

In class that day, we had been debating the hypothetical, but the concept of rape was very real to Lynsey. I wrapped my arms around her while she cried into my shoulder in the girls' restroom. I listened as the pain hit her all over again—the anger for justice still being so fresh, though she had managed to live without her best friend for four years now. . . .

I remember the way the sun warmed our classroom and the arrangement of our desks in the room, and I remember the way Lynsey wore her hair that day, because it was the first image that flashed through my mind when I found out, two years later, that she herself had become another victim of rape and a brutal murder.

I vividly remember the day I learned about Lynsey's death too. It was a Sunday morning at 10:00 a.m. My phone rang.

"Did you hear?"

I failed to find words as I listened to my friend D break the news to me. His friend's father was a local cop, so I was finding out just moments before the story broke in our town. There's something strangely unsettling about being one of the first to know something tragic has happened. You wonder, *If I don't ever share this information, can I make it all go away?* Amid the deep sadness of the tragedy itself, you feel a sense of fault—as if you're somehow responsible for the news that's going to alter someone's life forever. The news made me sick to my stomach, and I ran to the bathroom and gagged.

I rushed to the gas station a mile from my house where my friend Katie was working the morning shift. I wondered if she knew what had happened. Everything was spinning.

I ran inside and knew by the expression on Katie's face that she had found out too. *Thank God I do not have to be the one who tells her.*

"A house fire?" I blurted, still stunned—not waiting politely until she was done checking someone out at the register. She met my eyes and gave the woman her change. "And she and her dad *both* died?" I was seeking answers because I had only gotten bits and pieces of information. It was like the game of telephone: Everyone's wording sounded a little bit different from the last person's. Had I heard the news correctly?

"It wasn't her dad in there with her, Lindsey." Her face saddened more. "There was another guy in there, but we don't know who yet. And the police are calling it a double homicide."

My mouth dropped open. Someone had done this to them. It wasn't an accident. "And they don't know *who* did this yet?" My hand covered my mouth. *Oh my God, it could be anyone.* My mind started shuffling through the names of drug dealers in our city who might have done this. You didn't have to buy their drugs to know who they were.

One by one, our girlfriends called us to ask for details we didn't yet know. Katie got out of her shift early, and we all met at her parents' house just down the street. Several of us wanted to be together while details emerged. We piled in the living room of her parents' home and stayed up all night. We took phone calls while we watched the news, trying to make sense of the death of our friend.

Several hours later, the manhunt ended. The news station plastered a picture of his face on the TV screen, right next to her senior picture—the one she loved and had eagerly passed out to all of us after they were printed. I had my own copy. Now her picture was displayed across every TV in the state of Indiana. I grappled with the reality that I would never hear her call my name again or feel her long slender arms wrap around my neck. I couldn't take my eyes off the picture of the scraggly haired man next to her. I didn't recognize him. *That man killed my friend. She is dead. He killed her.* I was trying to understand. I looked at her senior picture and wondered if she had tried to fight him.

We slept overnight at Katie's house. We didn't want to be alone. The next morning, my friends and I started gathering pictures to make a slideshow for the funeral. We knew we couldn't just sit around and cry; we had to do something. Each of us drove home in search of all the pictures we could find.

I pulled in the driveway of my parents' house and ran inside. My mom and dad were both awake and sitting in the living room. I hadn't spoken to them much since I found out about Lynsey's death. I felt worlds away from them. *They don't understand*, I concluded. They probably didn't know what to say either. It was all so surreal. I ran upstairs to my room, opening every drawer I kept my loose photos in. I pulled out all my pictures and riffled through them, but I wanted to get back to my friends. I decided it would take too much time to go through photo albums too, so I just stacked the albums in my arms and carried them to the car.

I ran back downstairs and looked into the living room. "I'm going back to Katie's. I'll be there all day and night." My parents just listened to me. I can only imagine how concerned they must have been, but they let me go without any hesitation. I don't remember seeing them again until the funeral.

My friends and I put the slideshow of pictures together and sent it to the funeral home. We hand-selected a playlist too—all songs attached to memories of Lynsey. Songs like "Count on Me" by Whitney Houston and CeCe Winans, "Dirty Diana" by Michael Jackson, "I'll Be There," and "When You Believe" by Mariah Carey and Whitney Houston—to name a few. I still can't listen to any of these songs today without thinking of her.

At the funeral home, my friends and I met in the parking lot before walking in. We went early, before the crowd would arrive, though the place was already full of her grieving family. I walked into the room and immediately eyed the casket. I spotted the top of her head from the back of the room. I wasn't sure before arriving if it would be an open casket or a closed one. *God, please don't let me see it.* I prayed if it was open that I would not see the cut on her neck.

A friend looped her arm in mine and asked if I'd walk up to see Lynsey with her. I'd never have said no. We were all in this together. We walked up to the front of the room, and the closer we got, the less the body looked like my friend—making it easier to deny that it was actually her, dead in that wooden box. I thought back to the last time I saw her: a casual run-in at the gas station. She called my name as she was getting back in her car and I was walking inside. I ran over to her and gave her a big hug. I hadn't seen her in over a year. She and I went our separate ways that night.

I looked at her hands, folded on top of each other like she was resting peacefully. *Her hands look so yellow.* I moved my eyes to her face, which held all her light while she was alive. I didn't recognize her without her smile. "Hey, Lynz," I tried to say, but it felt so abnormal to speak to a body that wouldn't speak back. Her chin touched her chest, and I knew they'd done that on purpose so no one could see the wound.

I read a sign above the casket that said: "Please do not touch the bodies." I didn't obey. I placed my hand on the top of her head and rubbed my fingers gently over her hair. It was smooth to the touch, as if it had been brushed for hours. I let the strands of her silky, dirty blond hair fall through my fingers, and I remembered how I used to watch her so gracefully twist and knot the strands of her hair in class when she was bored. "Teach me how you do that!" I'd whisper to her so our teacher wouldn't hear us talking. She spent a whole free period teaching me, and I would never forget it.

I focused on what I was feeling as I ran my hand over her head. I wanted to remember it forever. Sometimes, even today, while I'm running my fingers through my own hair, I'll sense the same silky feeling, and it catches me off guard. I always stop to take notice, giving that moment to Lynsey. Sometimes, I'll even close my eyes while I search for the silkiest strand of hair on my own head so I can be transported back to that memory. But it's not painful in the memory; I am just happy to be next to her again.

I observed again how her hands crossed over each other, and I laid my hand on top of them. They were cold and bony, and I felt the grit of whatever makeup they used to cover the parts of her body we were all seeing for the very last time. I didn't let my hand linger over hers long, because the lifelessness was starting to make me feel sick. I'd had all I could handle.

The funeral went as one might expect. There weren't many words exchanged. Only tears, falling in unison.

The days following her funeral consisted of messy grief amid my tight circle of girlfriends. We were all unsure how to move on. We did the best we could, leaning on our vices of liquor and mindlessness, drinking until we'd fall asleep. It worked for a while—until it didn't.

I paused to see if Jen was still listening. She was tracking my words with a pen in hand and a notebook on her lap.

"I wanted to run away."

Jen nodded as if that desire was understandable.

"So, I kind of did. At nineteen years old, four months after Lynsey died, I called my friends together and told them I was moving.

"I quit thinking about Indiana. It was the only way I knew how to move forward. Tennessee became my safe place. It was refreshing. Vibrant. Bustling with people all moving toward a better life. There was no history or trauma attached to my life in Tennessee. I could be whoever I wanted to be. I could create a new life and forget about the pain."

"Are you still in contact with your friends and family back home?" Jen asked.

"I am, but I carry a lot of guilt for leaving them. I'm caught between two very different worlds."

I looked down at my daughter sitting at my feet, still playing with her toys. How did she stay so entertained?

Jen set down her notebook. "I'm not sure that's your guilt to carry, Lindsey. But we'll talk more about that later." She told me that our time had ended. "I'm glad you're here," she said.

I looked at the clock. I'd been talking for almost two hours. I couldn't believe how quickly the time had passed.

We stood, and she offered me a hug. I folded myself into her arms, not knowing how much I had needed the comfort. Then I picked up my daughter and gathered up her toys, and Jen showed us out.

"You look . . . lighter," Jonathan said as I walked through the front door. He eyed me with curiosity. I watched his puzzled face take in a change in my demeanor. But I dismissed his observations and set our daughter down, then walked over and embraced him. I guess I did feel a bit weightless.

five

Darkness and a Dream

I joined my husband on the couch after putting our daughter to bed that night.

"Something on your mind?"

"A lot," I said cheekily, "but I don't want to talk about it right now." I scooted close to him and wedged myself underneath his arm. This didn't happen often, but sometimes if we were in a neutral zone—a moment when sex was less likely to take place—I could get out of my own head enough to desire to be touched.

Will Jen leave me when she finds out? She doesn't know the whole story yet. I talked myself in and out of a doubt spiral, sure there was a condition to Jen's desire to care for me. *What will she think of me when I tell her?* This was part of the process, I reminded myself: trusting that nothing would change when I told her I was attracted to women.

Trust is not an easy thing to earn. Not my trust, anyway.

After so much hurt, I kept people at arm's length. I wanted closeness but was so afraid of the moment the closeness would be taken away from me, so I figured it was safest to keep my distance. With Jen, I was already experiencing a kind of closeness. It was new, and it was healthy. I was afraid I would taint it.

Is it even worth it? Should I just not tell her?

I peeked at our daughter on my way to bed. We had recently bought our first house, and I was still getting used to her being in her own room. Maybe it was the way she tucked my old pillowcase, which she used as a blankie, underneath her cheek or how she laid in her bed so peacefully, but seeing her sound asleep set my heart at ease. In this moment, I felt wildly sufficient as a mother, able to give her a quiet place to rest with a blanket to hug—something nurturing, something I knew she needed.

My husband didn't like going to sleep at separate times, so he met me in bed. As much as his desire to be next to me sometimes turned me off (I had labeled him "clingy"), I was beginning to admire it. How he *still* wanted to be next to me felt noble. Especially after all I'd put us through. I saw the weariness in his eyes. I felt it, too, but it didn't affect his desire to be with me as much as it affected my desire to stay.

He moved in close, politely asking if he could put his arms around me. But it felt a little too close now that we were in the bedroom. I didn't want to tell him tonight that his touch was what caused me to lose my breath in anxiety—though maybe he knew it already, considering he would always ask for permission to hold me. He situated himself on the bed and pulled his body close to mine, curving his shape around me as I turned on my side, facing away from him. I felt his arms encircle me, one underneath my head and the other resting somewhat heavily on my rib cage. He breathed in relief, finding comfort in the closeness. I held my breath, counting the seconds until he'd let go.

I waited until he was asleep so I could maneuver out from beneath his love without waking him up. Free of his arms, I laid flat on my back, staring at the ceiling fan as it moved around again and again with the same speed and the same force. I let the repetitive spinning settle my thoughts.

I drifted off to sleep and began to dream.

I am standing in a field of tall grass and brown willows. I look around. I am alone. Something catches my attention from a distance, and I see him. A man, filled with darkness. This man is coming for me. My heart is beating fast. I want to move, but my legs are paralyzed. He takes a step closer to me. His eyes are on fire with hatred. His face is pale white—a stark contrast to his yellowish-brown, sharp teeth. His hair is wiry and unkempt, though the top of his head is mostly bald. He raises his arm and points his finger directly at me. I try to move again, but my feet will not budge. I am stuck in the field as this man pins me down with his murderous eyes.

"I'm coming for you," he says. When he speaks, his voice carries straight into my ear, as if he is intimately close. I panic. I am alone, and I have nowhere to go.

My breathing escalates as he begins to walk toward me, his pace quickening with each step. He starts to run. I try to yell, but I have no voice.

The image of his face moves in closer and closer, and I know it will be the end of me if he gets to me.

I jerked awake.

My body was frozen in fear. The fan continued to spin around and around in our bedroom, reminding me of where I was. I reached over and pulled the chain on the lamp.

I shook my husband awake and cried out for protection. "The man," was all I could say. "He's coming for me." My breathing was short. I was having an anxiety attack.

My husband tried to calm me, rubbing my back and telling me it was okay, that no man was coming for me. "It was just a bad dream, Lindsey."

"No, it was real. He is hunting me." I dismissed his comfort and pulled out my Bible. I started reading line after line of whatever I opened the pages to. I used to do this as a child, whenever I was afraid, as though the words were a shield against whoever or whatever was coming after me.

My breathing began to slow. *It was just a dream.* I tried hard to believe Jonathan's words. *I am safe.* It might have been only a dream, but it was the realest dream I'd ever had.

After nearly an hour of repeating psalms, cradled now in my husband's arms, my mind began to settle. I tugged on the lamp chain again and was finally ready to rest. A slight breeze made its way through our bedroom window, which was cracked just enough to help soothe me back to sleep.

I was nearing the moment my thoughts would drift off into a wave of rest when I was interrupted by what sounded like a wolf howling nearby.

Jonathan and I shot up in bed simultaneously, having both heard it. "Did you hear that?" I asked him.

"Yeah, I definitely heard that."

Again, I tugged the chain of our bedside lamp and climbed out of bed. This time, I was pissed. "I'm going out there, damnit."

"Where?" Jonathan asked, clearly questioning my reasons for confronting an actual wolf if the sound we heard was true to its nature.

"Outside. I don't know what's going on, but I'm not having this"—meaning I would not accept any spirit, ghost, or wolf trying to scare me. I felt exceptionally protective of my house, my space, and—most importantly—our daughter. I asked my husband to check on her, and I called for my dog to join me. He was a pit bull mix, loyal to his mom, so I felt invincible with him as reinforcement should my idea turn south.

Our daughter was sound asleep, thank God. Her innocence ignited my zealousness to guard her. Come wolf or demon, I would defeat it and protect our daughter's rest. In the morning she would wake peacefully, having never known I'd fought a war on her behalf. *I will handle this*, I thought.

I unlocked the back door, then stepped onto the deck and into the night. My dog trotted past me, running down the steps, then skipping the last one as he leapt into our backyard. He meandered for a moment, and though he saw no wolf, he found a bush to lift his leg and pee on—showcasing his indifference to my nightmare.

I fixed my eyes on the field behind our house, looking for threats. I felt powerful in my fearlessness.

After several minutes, I didn't hear another howl. Nor did I see the man in my dream intimidating me with his scowl and hatred—but I spoke to them both anyway. "I don't belong to you," I said with boldness, but quietly enough to not disturb my neighbors. "You will not come near me or my family again."

My dog ran back up the stairs and passed me to go back inside, but I lingered on the deck for a few more minutes.

I will not be taken out easily, I thought.

I came back inside and noticed my husband was just a few steps away, waiting for me in the kitchen. Protecting me. Knowing I needed to address the darkness on my own. This was my moment to claim, though he was never too far away.

I rolled over in bed. The clock read eight a.m. Our daughter was still asleep, a sign of grace after a night like the one Jonathan and I had had. I snuck around the house to the kitchen, looking for coffee, but we were out. Then I tiptoed back into the bedroom to let my husband know I was going to the store to get some. "The baby is still asleep," I said, "and if you get up now, you could catch the kickoff to the Manchester United match." I kissed him on the cheek before leaving.

As I drove, I replayed the nightmare in my mind. It felt significant still. Who was the man I saw? He looked like no one I knew. Even so, I could see his eyes shaped like blades, intent on taking me out. But then I thought about the field he stood in, the one that looked vaguely familiar.

I neared the grocery store and saw the Publix sign from the stoplight, but I turned the opposite way.

Instead I rolled through the streets of a bustling historic town on a Saturday morning. People were already out walking with coffee in hand, and I wondered how they had enough money to shop every weekend. But then I reminded myself of where we lived. I passed through a stoplight and came to a street that wrapped around the back of the town—behind the shops and the people. There was typically little motion on this street, but today there was none. Out there, I noticed it. A weedy field behind an old historic jail, with nothing behind the field but more weeds. Was this it? Yes, this was where he was standing. I slowly drove past the jail, carefully taking note of every corner. I saw no one there, yet I turned my car around and parked right in front of the abandoned building, facing the field behind it.

I repeated my mantra from the night before under my breath: "I will not be taken out easily." I was still ready to fight, but in a way that took out the darkness and no longer my husband.

I've pushed him enough.

I'd spent so many hours fighting the one who loved me the most, testing his love. Pushing him to the very breaking of himself, until he'd shout, "I don't know what you want, Lindsey! I am giving you everything I have." On those days I'd find Jonathan on the floor in tears. Like an addict to my own suffering, I'd apologize over and over again for the pain I'd caused him—pulling him in, begging him, "Please don't give up on me yet."

Now it was time to let go of the torment. The shame. The regret. It was time to fight the voice that said my life was worthless and that I'd be better off dead.

I put the car in drive, making sure I didn't forget to stop for coffee on my way back home.

six

Push/Pull

"They kicked the door down!" my dad yelled, inspecting the damaged side door leading into our home. I heard the anger in his voice. He stood in the doorframe, then bent down to pick up a piece of broken hinge. My mom, sister, and I stayed quiet in the car until told what to do next. I thought about our shy beagle mix pup and how she was inside during the robbery. I started to cry, "Mom, what if they hurt Penny?" She didn't answer.

After searching the house, my dad motioned for my mom to bring us inside. It was Christmastime and we'd been at my grandparents' house celebrating when someone decided to break in. They stole mostly beer and jewelry my mom rarely wore, but the saddest loss was the few presents they had taken from underneath our Christmas tree.

My dad was already on the phone with the police when I ran past him and called out for our dog. My sister and I frantically searched our small, two-bedroom home until I spotted her trying to wiggle her way out from beneath our living room couch. "Here she is!" I yelled. I ran over to Penny, and my sister scooped her up in her arms. I wondered how she had fit her body into that small of a space.

The police arrived, and my dad told them everything he knew. They rubbed something on the doorframe, and my mother told me it was because they were trying to get the fingerprints of whoever did this—though the police "could not promise" us they'd ever find out, I heard the officer say. He didn't sound optimistic.

The culprit left dirty shoe prints underneath our beds, which was especially terrifying for a child who was already afraid of what was under her bed at night. "But how did the footprints get there?" I asked repeatedly because no one seemed to hear me. While those in the house still searched for clues, I was visualizing intruders crawling around like demons: low and quiet, bending like contortionists, waiting until I was all covered up in bed to snatch me. My dad finally stopped and answered me: "They flipped the beds over to see if anything of value was under them." My young mind now envisioned them less as demons and more like big guys who wouldn't be able to sneak around as easily. Still, I didn't want to be alone in my bedroom.

I watched the police officer take notes on his yellow notepad. He looked down at me and smiled. "Who's this little guy?"

My mom moved in close and put her hand on my head. "This is Lindsey."

The officer addressed his mistake quickly, realizing I was not a little guy at all. "Oh! I'm sorry!" Maybe they thought I didn't notice that he called me a boy, but I did. I ran my fingers through my hair, wondering if his mistake was my fault because my hair wasn't pretty enough.

The police officer finished discussing matters with my parents and promised to be in touch. The hinges had been destroyed, so while my dad tried to stabilize the door for the night, my mom walked my sister and me to our bedrooms to find our pajamas. I stayed close by her leg, not wanting to be too far away from her. My mom told us we'd be sleeping with her that night, and I wouldn't be in my room all alone. My sister and I found a spot on our parents' bed, and my mom pulled the blankets up over us. Penny jumped up on the bed, curling her little body into a tight circle at our feet. Mom kissed us both and said she'd be right back.

"Will you leave the light on, Mom?" . . .

"They never did find out who broke in." I shrugged my shoulders as if it wasn't that big of a deal anymore.

As I recounted this memory to Jen, I became less inclined to talk about the trauma of the break-in and more curious about the police officer's comment. Had that been the spark of an identity confusion that stayed with me throughout my childhood—attaching itself to the notion that if I were pretty enough, I wouldn't be mistaken for a boy? This humiliation hurt me deeper than the robber had by stealing our Christmas presents.

"I began to obsess over the details of how I looked, especially the older I got." I never knew *how* to become more pretty, so I'd just watch the ways my older sister's pretty friends would move and laugh and flirt. When I was alone in my room, I'd practice what I'd observed and watch myself in the mirror. I concluded that being pretty was a lot of work.

"I don't think I'm pretty." I was honest with Jen, and the surprise of my own vulnerability hit me in the gut. "There are days when I hate myself so much I'll just stare in the mirror until I find a reason to hate myself even more."

"Lindsey." The way she said my name forced me to look up from the floor and meet her eyes. "You are a very beautiful woman." I shrugged it off. I remembered another friend saying something similar to me after I told her how ugly I thought I was. We were on a walk, and she interrupted me. "You're going to have to stop thinking that." But it wasn't a matter of just *stopping*. It had been an identity. Even my own husband's unashamed attraction for me—that he never failed to show through his body language and words—couldn't dismantle the belief I'd held for so long.

"I used to hear these voices in my mind, constantly reminding me of how worthless and ugly I was." Sometimes I'd even beat myself in the head with my hairbrush when the tangles didn't come out.

"Tell me what you heard," she prompted.

"At first, there weren't any words. The noise would start out like a volume dial slowly turning up louder and louder in my ears. It was a pestering loudness that wouldn't go away. But it was all in my head, never any real sound.

"I never had control over when it would come or go," I continued, "but it was usually when I was still or winding down at night. It would end up so loud I had to press my hands tightly over my ears. The sounds mimicked someone screaming at me in a rage, but only I could hear it."

Jen took notes, but not in way that disconnected her from the story. She was present, listening closely.

"This torment made me feel like I was never wanted. I sensed I needed to earn my love, because I wasn't good enough for it as I was."

"How so?"

"I felt like I was to blame . . . for everything. I can't pinpoint a memory attached to *why* I felt that way, but I felt like I was the one responsible for keeping my mom and dad alive. I carried the belief that if I did anything wrong, my mistake would kill my parents."

"That is a heavy burden to carry, Lindsey."

Clearly, I was realizing, there was something deeper here. I'd even shocked myself by saying it out loud. "As I got older, those voices led to a standard of perfection I held myself to. If I was running on the treadmill, I'd turn the speed up as fast as I could go, and I'd still hear, 'Faster, or your mother will die.' Sounds extreme as I say it now, but it was normal for me as a child."

I paused and let my attention drift to the beauty outside the windows. I inhaled slowly, taking as much oxygen in as possible. As I exhaled, there was a tiredness to it. The sigh indicated a long road of healing ahead. It was also hard to be reminded of a little girl who felt so deeply lost and alone.

Jen broke the silence. "Did you ever share any of this with your family?"

"I didn't. I felt embarrassed by it. I was afraid there was something seriously wrong with me, so I told myself it was better not to mention it. It was easier to fight the voices the best I knew how and just hope that one day they would go away."

Jen stayed quiet while I processed out loud.

"But I don't think staying hidden has helped me—at all, obviously." I gestured to the fact that I was now sitting in her office as my life unraveled before me. "Not sharing the pain with my parents really began to affect my relationship with them over time."

"I imagine it did," Jen said. "You were taking on a lot of responsibility for such a young girl."

Her comment made me feel seen, as though she cared. I was finally getting to experience some relief from bringing up all the memories I'd kept tucked away for so long. Someone else finally knew, and it was liberating not to be the only one holding onto a childhood of secrets. Of course, I had pain to face, traveling back into the world I escaped from, but it didn't feel so impossible a task when I knew I wouldn't face it alone. Jen's tenderness guided me; I would go as deep as her empathy would lead.

seven

Monticello

My first childhood home was a little blue house. It was perched on top of a hill, in a neighborhood that bordered low-income apartments and a 911 call station. The hill was perfect for sledding, something my older sister and I often enjoyed during those snowy Midwest winters.

I loved our humble blue home. Just behind it was the street that took me to my best friend Megan's house. On those warm summer days, we'd spend our evenings running in between backyards, getting into the purest kinds of mischief. But on the weekends, my family and I would visit my grandparents' lake cottage.

It always felt like it took a lifetime to get to the lake house, but really the drive was just under two hours. We were usually the first to arrive, after my grandparents. If I'd been napping in the car, I'd wake up instantly at the sound of our tires running over the gravel road that led us back to the one-street neighborhood of permanently placed mobile homes. Even now, the sound of driving on a gravel road takes me back there. We'd unload and I'd run through the cottage, looking in every room like it was a new house. It always felt good to be back.

More of our family would show up as the hours went on. Aunts and uncles, cousins, and sometimes our family dogs all made their way to the cottage where we'd spend unforgettable days swimming, tubing, boating, and eating. We never failed to eat with my Mimi being there. She was the captain of our crew, always planning our meals together. She'd send my Papaw to pick blackberries in the weeds so she could make pie later that night. I went with him one morning and stood on the dock while he scaled a hill of poison ivy to get Mimi her blackberries. I chuckled as he struggled. His silliness was infectious, and I loved being around him.

Early one morning, while most were still asleep, I woke up and saw my mother grabbing her ski vest. My grandpa was up with her, and I knew what they were going to do. I quickly found my own life jacket, still hanging over a lawn chair, drying from the day before, and asked if I could come along.

Mornings were perfect for skiing. The lake was smooth, fully recovered from the recreation of Jet Skis, tubers, and speedboats from the day before. I took my Papaw's hand as he helped me into his red speedboat. My mom untied the ropes from the dock.

We didn't go far, just out past the weeds, before my mom zipped up her life jacket and jumped in the water. Papaw threw her the skis, and she wiggled her feet into the holds. My job was to untangle the knots in the ski rope—quickly, too, because even though the boat was in neutral, we were still gliding. I tossed the rope out to my mom just as she finished setting her feet.

She situated the rope between her legs and pointed her long, skinny skis out of the water. Sitting her butt back, she wrapped her fingers around the bar attached to the rope knotted to the back of our boat. Papaw looked at me. "You ready, Linds?" he asked, knowing as soon as my mom yelled "Go!" he'd have to floor it. I loved when he called me Linds. There was something playful about it, like I was his buddy as much as I was his granddaughter.

I grabbed hold of the metal bar beside my seat for extra stability. "I'm ready, Papaw!"

He turned around to face my mom and hollered, "Ready?" His voice echoed across the easy tempered water like there was not another sound at this moment on the big, beautiful lake.

It's just us out here. I enjoyed the solitude.

"Go!" I heard her yell. He pushed the throttle down to full speed.

Sit back. Elbows straight. Keep your knees bent. I reminded myself the three keys to getting up on the first try as I watched the white wake billow behind the boat.

In those first few moments of takeoff, everyone was focused. It was a lesson in timing. At exactly the right moment, my mother's skill would need to match the power of the boat. She could either stand—with help—or miss the moment and lose her ability to hold onto the bar attached to the rope. *Keep your elbows straight, Mom. Keep your knees bent, and lean back.*

I watched her go from underwater to riding the wake in a matter of seconds. Once she stood up, she rode the waves with ease, and for laps around the lake, like a Sunday cruise. I sat back and enjoyed the wind tousling my hair as I watched my mother come to life.

The faster Papaw drove, the more comfortable my mom would get, steadying herself against the traction on her skis. Speed made it easier for her to stand, like a strong arm helping her up. It was a team effort.

My mom was a middle school teacher, so I got to spend all my summers, weeknights, and weekends with her. She never missed a holiday or family function or sporting event. She made us family dinners every night and helped us with our homework. Sometimes I got to grade papers with her, which was one of my favorite things to do because I got to hold *the* red pen that all teachers used for corrections. She was always present. My safe place.

I spent a few years beneath the wing of my mother. Never really wanting to leave her side. I was always most comfortable when she was home. But as the years went by, and the harder life became to navigate on my own, the more I distanced myself from my parents. I wanted to be independent of their authority but still live in their house—which doesn't work out well for most teenagers.

I remember the time, as a young teenager, when I was sure I'd just experienced the "last straw" moment between my parents and me. I stomped up the stairs to my bedroom in a total rage, then glared down at my mother. I looked her directly in the eyes, absent of any emotion other than the fury I carried, and aimed to cut her with my words: "I hate you." She said nothing in return. I thought being apathetic to her feelings would make my loathing cut deeper, but her demeanor showed neither pain nor frustration—only exhaustion. I went to my room and slammed my door shut. Only then, behind closed doors, did I break apart. I fell to my knees in silent tears.

I never knew how to talk to my parents about my insecurities, my creeping depression, or my suicidal thoughts when the middle school bullying got so bad. I thought my pain would cause them sadness, and that emotion was worse than any other pain I could cause them—even anger. I could handle my parents getting angry or grounding me, but seeing them sad, even on behalf of something I was the victim of, was too much shame for me to handle. So, I told myself it was better to just cut ties with my parents. I concluded that needing them was more painful than not.

eight

Belonging

"I need to talk about second grade," I told Jen. Something about that year of my life felt pressing—monumental to the way I presented myself as an adult.

I was still finding my way as a mother, wondering how I would protect my daughter and what role I would play in her life. I carried this identity now, having someone so small and helpless completely dependent on me. Some days this scared me. How could God entrust such a beautiful, tenderhearted soul to my care? I knew she would break one of these days, because everyone does, but when she did, I wanted it to be a *normal* type of breaking—like when your crush likes someone else or you fight with best friend for the first time. I would do everything in my power to make sure her first heartbreak didn't come from a grown-up's abusive behavior—as it had, in my case, from my elementary school teacher.

My daughter was barely a toddler. As fast as the first year

of her life had gone, I knew it would not be long before I was making school lunches and writing notes to place inside her lunch box. I couldn't imagine her having to face the loneliness I faced during the second grade—that crucial year of my life.

"As I think about it now, all I feel is anger," I told Jen.

"It must have impacted you pretty significantly."

"It did, but it's surprising to me that I feel the need to bring it up now. I haven't thought about it in a long time. Sometimes I wonder if it really happened. I wonder how a teacher could be so mean." I felt my voice crack. Perhaps this wasn't such a distant memory after all, but one I carried right beneath the surface. Potentially, this was the one story that could lead me back to the moment I first learned to hide my true self and silence my true emotions. The moment I learned that happiness meant compliance and sadness meant trouble.

"I feel nervous to recount the story." I held my hands together and placed them in my lap. Jen allowed for the silence, knowing it would take me a minute to start. I felt the tightness in my throat from the sadness trying to surface.

"Whenever you're ready." She was assuring me that I was in a safe space, that I could be vulnerable here.

"I just missed my mom . . . that was all."

I processed aloud, trying to understand the reason I was treated so poorly. I was only a young girl.

"I missed her, and I cried about it on the first day of school, then the second day of school, and I couldn't stop no matter how hard I tried. The loneliness hit me like a punch in the stomach every time I got on the bus in the mornings." I continued unpacking the story. "My teacher, she hated me for the crying."

"How so?"

I pushed her question aside for a minute, careful not to break the train of thought.

"I remember initially being excited for school, picking out my outfit for the first day the night before, and taking a picture that morning with my new folder that had a white kitten on it. It makes me sad to think about it now, because it just feels like a piece of my heart was crushed that year of my life. I was never the same after it." I drew a breath and kept going.

"On the first day of school, I walked into the room and looked for my name tag on my assigned desk. There was a sense of comfort when I found my name, feeling like I belonged to something when everything else was new. I unloaded my backpack and put folders and pencils in their proper place. I didn't know many kids in my class and was really disappointed that my best friend didn't get the same teacher as I did. As the other kids filled in their seats, I waited patiently. My teacher had her back to us, writing her name in cursive on the large chalkboard above her desk.

"After the bell rang and the morning announcements came across the speakers, our teacher made us get out our folders and a pencil to write with. Maybe it was how my items smelled of home or the memory of back-to-school shopping with my mom just a few nights earlier, but the change of a summer ending and school starting made me feel homesick.

"I remember burying my face in my arms as the tears

started to fall. The classroom was silent except for my crying. And then I heard a stern voice call out to me. 'What's the matter?' I poked my head up, startled that I had been discovered. I rubbed my eyes with my hands and said, 'I miss my mom.'

"Well, Mrs. B dismissed my reasoning abruptly and said, 'If you don't quit crying, I'll put you in the hallway.'

"Her tone and her temper scared me. I'd never been in trouble at school before. My stomach curled and my crying grew louder, her hardness causing me to be more homesick than I was before. 'Go ahead,' she said, pointing to the door. 'You can sit in the hallway until you're finished. You're disrupting my class.'

"I slid out of my desk and saw my classmates staring at me. She walked me to the hallway, pointed to a spot on the floor just outside of her door, and told me to sit. So, I sat down and pulled my knees up to my chest. I folded my arms and hid my face. Then she said, 'When you're done crying, come in and find your seat.'

"From where I was sitting, I could see my best friend in the classroom next to us. She was smiling as her teacher gave friendly instruction. I tried to catch her eyes, but her gaze was fixed, and I remember wondering if I could ask my parents if I could switch classes. But then her teacher walked over to the open door and pushed it shut. She never even poked her head out in the hallway to check on the little girl sitting there by herself. The door just rolled off her fingers and slammed shut.

"The next day, I cried again. I begged my dad to keep me home, but he threatened me with trouble if I didn't go to school. I missed the bus that morning because I wouldn't come out of the bathroom." I chuckled at my defiance. This wasn't a funny story, of course, but thinking about the stubbornness of little Lindsey made me kind of proud.

"What happened the next day?" Jen asked.

"It got even worse," I continued. "I sat in the hallway until I stopped crying, but when I walked back into the room, she wouldn't let me sit down. I tried to quietly sneak back into class and not bother anyone, but she called me up front right as I entered." I looked away from Jen, trying to recount the memory as best as I could. "She went around the room, asking each kid to tell me what they thought about my crying. But she didn't encourage kindness; she wanted them to tell me how I was disrupting them. I can still see their faces. Most of them didn't want to say anything. Actually, I don't remember a lot of what they said, except for two of them."

"What did they say, Lindsey?" Jen crossed her legs and leaned back. It made me feel loved that she cared about the details so much.

"The first kid, he was a boy—and it was only the boys' comments that I remember. He said, 'I think she should stop crying and just know that she'll see her mom when she gets home.' I can still hear it today.

"Mrs. B affirmed him. 'Good!' she said, then pointed to the next kid. She moved from kid to kid until she called on my friend Matt. He was a friend from my neighborhood that I spent most summer days with. 'It doesn't bother me,' he said, with the same kindness that I'd experienced all summer. 'If she misses her mom, then I think it's okay for her to cry.' I lifted my eyes from the floor and cracked a smile his way. His defense surprised me."

"Sounds like he cared for you," Jen affirmed.

"He did. I feel like it was a bold thing for a kid to say. But I wish it would have stopped there. After she went around the room, she took her disgust for my emotion further and taught the class a song they'd sing to me. You know the birthday song, right? Well, she changed the lyrics but kept the same tune, spelling out the letters B-A-B-Y as the only lyric to the whole song."

I witnessed Jen become unsettled as I sang the song back to her. Usually, her responses were held together, but this story seemed to bother her. Maybe it was because she had a daughter in second grade and couldn't imagine her enduring such a heavy load of shame from her schoolteacher.

"Lindsey, wow. I am very sorry you were treated this way." Jen extended compassion, but I was new at knowing how to accept it. I shrugged my shoulders like it wasn't a big deal, but clearly my emotions said otherwise.

"How did your parents respond to this?" She was following the thread, trying to find where it still attached to my heart today.

"They didn't because I didn't tell them. Are you seeing a pattern?" I said dryly. "I thought I would be the one in trouble if they found out. As a mother now myself, it makes me sad that I never told my mom or my dad after this happened."

I got by as best as I could in that classroom. I never cried in class again, not after that humiliating song. Not only had this teacher hurt my feelings in a way that fractured the innocence of a seven-year-old little girl, but she did it by tainting one of my favorite songs—one tied explicitly to a day of joy and excitement.

I could still trace the scent of her perfume and how quickly it gave me a headache upon entering her room. I remembered the way she tied her long, gray hair up in a messy bun that always sat lopsided on the top of her head. I remembered her large, rimmed glasses and her long, beaded jewelry. I remembered our classroom project when we were asked to bring in our favorite stuffed animal for an exchange program with a child in Europe. We sent our animals to live there for a month until they were returned to us with letters from our pen pals. I remembered how excited everyone was the day the package arrived—yet my bear wasn't inside. I remembered telling my teacher that mine was gone and how she did not seem to care. I remembered wanting to cry, but that I didn't.

Reliving these moments was bringing up a lot of emotion. Even the best memories still carried a tinge of sadness with them.

"May I take a little break?"

"Sure you can." Jen set her notebook down and stood up as I did.

I walked outside and ventured into her backyard, admiring the trees lined in rows next to each other. The leaves were alive with color. I was anxious to roam.

The sounds of autumn wrestled under my feet as I shuffled

through the leaves. I was alone, but I felt alive. The way the trees moved reminded me of a choir: each movement like its own instrument, all singing in harmony. I felt the invitation to join along. I closed my eyes and felt the sun break through the chill to warm my cheeks. *I wonder if this is what it feels like to belong to something.* Outside of Jen, the sun was my most constant friend through this healing process. Always warming me, letting me know she was there to comfort.

I thought again about that year in school and wondered, *God, did you even notice?* God felt a lot like my teacher, pointing out my imperfections and making a mockery out of me: *You'll never be good enough, no matter how hard you try.* With my eyes closed, I visualized Mrs. B's look of disappointment, the sound of the door slamming, the song, and my missing bear.

I sat down in the grass, pulled my knees up to my chest, and rested my arms on them. *God, where were you?* I closed my eyes and drew my attention away from the present moment. I envisioned a man sitting next to me with his knees pulled up to his own chest, just like mine. I quickly opened my eyes, but I was still in Jen's backyard. I closed my eyes again to get a better look at the man, as if it were a dream I was trying to get back to. It didn't work. I couldn't see him anymore.

Slightly frustrated, I stood up and brushed the leaves off my jeans. I put my hands inside the pockets of my sweatshirt and looked up at the clouds. The sun touched my forehead with a kiss. "I see you," I said. I knelt down and ran my fingers through the grass. It, too, was alive.

I walked back inside, feeling thankful for the time alone.

Jen was straightening up her office space, throwing away the dirty tissues that I'd left on the ground. I was embarrassed to see her touching my snotty Kleenex. She smiled. "You seem a little lighter," she said, like there was a visible heaviness I'd been carrying around.

"Yeah, I feel a little better." I grabbed a pen and asked for a sheet of paper so I could jot down some notes about what I had seen while sitting outside. I wrote about the trees, the leaves, the sun on my skin, the disappointment, the isolation I felt in the hallway that day in the second grade, and the humiliation I felt while my class made fun of me in unison. I had shared the memory; now I was ready to let it go and leave it behind. Besides, I felt guilty for feeling so brokenhearted about my past when God had given me the sun and the trees. He'd also given me a great husband and our little girl.

I wrote out a prayer to God, but it was more like an apology for not being more present with what he'd already given me. What else had I missed already? *Oh, God, I am sorry for sucking at everything.* But then I wondered if this apology letter was about me—again—being too hard on myself. Maybe God wasn't mad at me for being broken. Maybe he wasn't scolding me like I was always scolding myself.

Back home, I pulled the folded-up sheet of paper from my back pocket and went to lie on the twin-sized bed we'd kept in our office. The house was quiet. I appreciated the moments when my husband would take our daughter out so I could get a few hours of solitude.

I laid on top of the covers, placing one hand on my chest and the other on my stomach, and focused on learning how to breathe in sync with the beat of my heart. I noticed when I drew in a long breath, filling up my belly, that the beat would slow down slightly, giving rest to an anxious heart and an overworked mind.

I focused on the silence of the room, my breath, and a body that was still giving me life. I was overcome with peace, as if someone was covering me with a weighted blanket—starting at my toes, moving over my legs, laying the covers gently over my body, stopping just under my neck. I took another deep inhale.

I thought about the loneliness that I wrestled with as a little girl. How grief manifested into rage, and how powerful my rage eventually made me feel. I looked up at the wall next to our bed and noticed the patched hole next to the light switch. Just days ago, I'd put another hole in our wall in a wave of anger. *I can't look at this.* I closed my eyes, remembering how scared my toddler was when she walked into the bedroom right as I took a swing into the drywall. I couldn't get the image of her precious, fear-filled face out of my mind. *I have to heal, or I will lose them both.* I was praying, or maybe it sounded more like pleading.

An hour later, I woke to the sound of my daughter calling my name in excitement. She and her dad had just gotten back, bringing dinner home with them too. I had fallen asleep on the twin mattress during my breath work. "I'm in here, babe." I tried to yell so she could find me, but I was still groggy. Jonathan walked in, and our daughter ran in behind him, trying to scale the bed to reach me. I leaned over and pulled her up onto my chest. She laid her head on me, and it melted away all the guilt held onto by a not-good-enough mother (or so I believed myself to be).

I sat up when my husband handed me a bag with a chicken sandwich inside it. "I remembered extra pickles. Which is so gross. I don't know how you eat those," he said in disgust. I rolled my eyes but thanked him for the food.

I pointed to the patch on the wall. "I need to finish painting that," I told him before I took a bite.

"I can paint it tomorrow when I get home from work," he said.

Why would he do that? He isn't the one who punched the hole in the wall. "No, I'll do it. You didn't cause this mess. I did." I hated the rage. I wanted it gone so badly. I wanted to be able to choose differently, and not immediately fight when triggered by the fear of being unlovable.

He put his hand on my back. "It's okay, Lindsey. We'll get it fixed up."

Why is he always so understanding?

Jonathan never held my mistakes over my head. He didn't have a tally sheet of my screwups, and he didn't make me feel like I owed him anything in return for his grace. He would not shy away from conversations about how difficult my rage episodes were for him, but he wouldn't let me die in my shame either. I never hurt him or our daughter. The pain was always inflicted toward myself, though it would be ignorant of me to conclude that self-inflicted wounds only inflicted *self.* Once, after our daughter was asleep, my rage turned into a panic attack, and my husband embraced the punches by holding me tightly in his arms until I calmed down. It took several minutes until I broke into tears and my body quit fighting. I laid in his arms until I had no more tears left to cry, and then he cried too.

Rage held the power to make me feel safe, which was why it was so hard for me to let go of it. But I knew it couldn't stay. I didn't want my daughter to see her mom explode like I had. I wanted more for her, more for Jonathan, and more for myself. The root of my rage ran deep. It took hold a long time ago, sown directly into the heart of a fragile little girl who was so terribly afraid she would never be good enough to be loved.

But the truth was there. Jonathan did love me, and he wanted me, but it would take more than that to heal. I needed to figure out how to love myself first.

nine

Holy Water

"I had this experience one summer," I told Jen. "I honestly still don't really know what to think about it. I just remember showing up to church camp with my best friend, and after the first or second night, I was told I was possessed by a demon and needed an exorcism."

I focused my attention on the details of the books she had stacked in her office, trying to home in on the memories. "Then I remember being in a field, facing a man who was significantly taller than me, standing as quiet as I could as he yelled at the demon and poured holy water on my head."

Jen's expression was puzzled. Clearly, she was curious to know more. I recounted it as best as one could with a traumatizing experience.

It was the summer before seventh grade. My parents dropped me off at the parking lot where the Greyhound bus waited to take my best friend, Elise, and me to church camp. I waved goodbye to them and ran with my bags across the parking lot to hug my friend. We shoved our bags underneath the bus, squishing them snugly together to fit with all the other bags. Everyone seemed to be in a frantic hurry to get the bus moving. Maybe we were all just excited about a week of independence.

I ran up the steps and found a spot toward the front of the bus for Elise and me. We were not fans of the back of the bus, where boys made strange fart noises and girls pretended not to notice them. She and I were lost in our own world of pop culture and boy band gossip, and we were comforted by each other's presence. We were more like sisters than friends.

The bus ride was long and loud, as one might expect from a bus full of preteens and tweens. Every now and then, my mind would trail off as I'd watch the trees race past us outside the bus window. I would try to lock my eyes on just one branch as we flew past it. Everything was so green now, *finally.* In Indiana, spring lasted well into May, and the trees were not in full bloom until at least the middle of the month. By summertime, though, the leaves turned a rich, healthy green. The trees comforted me, as I had already started to feel a little homesick.

I was relieved to finally see the entrance to the camp. The bus driver reminded us all to stay seated, as most of the kids in the back had stood up to get a better view of the grounds. I took note of the basketball courts and the swimming pool, where I planned to spend most of my time.

There were not many rules at camp, and we were free to use the unscheduled hours however we liked. Like at most summer camps, we had a myriad of activities to choose from—so many activities that by the end of the week, we were looking forward to returning to boredom. After we arrived, we had an hour of free time before we had to meet in the dining hall for lunch. Elise and I raced to the pool, and I cannonballed in to make her laugh.

The only true structure this camp had was to meet at the outdoor pavilion for singing worship songs, dancing, and praying after dinner. Rows of wooden chairs were lined up next to each other, facing the platform where the guitars were already staged. Soon the pastors or camp counselors—whatever they called themselves—walked onstage and encouraged the crowd of kids to get excited for Jesus. I admired them onstage, playing their guitars and mimicking a rock concert for God. Then, they slowed the beat down, and we were instructed to raise our hands and sing a new song called "Shout to the Lord."

When the music was over, we had thirty minutes of small group time. We were told to pick a group of three friends and head out to the large grassy area next to the worship pavilion. The camp was lined with trees, so we were in our own little retreat area, with no trace of the road or the outside world. My best friend and I found another girl we knew, and we picked a spot in the grass to sit on together. No one seemed too excited about this part of the evening, so we were promised a game of flashlight tag after it was over.

Each group was assigned a college-aged group leader—the

idea being that if hard things came up during our time of talking, she would be there to help guide us back to God. Our leader crisscrossed her legs, clasped her hands together, and told us this was a time we could talk about *anything.* Nothing was too difficult for God. She asked who wanted to talk first. I looked around the group and volunteered, knowing neither Elise nor our friend would be eager to go first.

I searched my thoughts to find something *serious* to talk about. (That's what it seemed like our counselor wanted.) Everyone was waiting for me to speak.

"I've not really told anyone about this, but sometimes I hear voices in my head, and they tell me I'm not a good person." Mentioning this made me feel embarrassed; I'd assumed I was the only one this ever happened to. Even so, I was surprised at how good it felt to say it out loud.

Our friend sitting across from me gently spoke up: "Me too."

I was shocked. "You've heard voices too?" She nodded her head yes, and we began to go back and forth explaining to each other what the voices sounded like. Mostly, what we felt was shame—both having no idea how to be better than we were. We felt the weight of the world, and all we cared about, on our shoulders.

"Sometimes I just feel afraid I'm going to do something wrong and like . . ." I struggled to say it because it felt so dumb. "Like my mistake will really hurt my mother or something."

My friend spoke up. "Yeah, I just feel like I hear that I'm not doing anything right."

We got lost in conversation because it was so easy to talk

to each other. Elise sat next to me, listening, probably hoping we'd keep talking until it was time to play flashlight tag.

Our group counselor uncrossed her legs and abruptly stood up. "I'll be right back," she said. I could hear the anxiety in her tone. Had we said too much?

The night was dark, but the pavilion glowed with old Christmas lights they'd repurposed for summer. A soft light reflected off our faces, and the three of us sat and waited until the counselor returned. We were no longer in deep conversation, just talking like twelve-year-old girls do—occasionally swatting at our arms and legs to squish the mosquitos that were making their presence known. Other kids were starting to leave their group time and run back to the pavilion, where we were instructed to meet before picking teams for flashlight tag.

The three of us stood, and I brushed the grass off the back of my shorts. I noticed our counselor on her way back toward us. She had brought a guy with her. The looks on their faces were concerning as they called me over to them. I wondered if I'd done something wrong. The guy addressed me and asked for more details about the voices I heard in my head. I explained it to him the best way I knew how. I looked around at my friends who had waited for me, just a few steps away.

The guy stepped forward and put his arm around my shoulder, like one does to a buddy. "This might sound scary, but Lindsey, we think you have a demon inside of you."

What does he mean? I was caught off guard by his words.

He looked me in the eyes and stated with boldness, "It needs to come out."

What was I supposed to say in response? I had watched *The Exorcist* in the third grade when I spent the night at my friend's house. Her dad was a film guru, and we found the scariest VHS he owned and popped it in the player after her parents went to bed. I could hardly sleep that night after watching it. But in this moment, I wasn't turning my head in circles like the possessed girl in the movie. I didn't understand what they meant by "demon," but I didn't ask any questions either. They instructed me and my two friends to come with them.

"When this is over, can we still play flashlight tag?" I asked.

"There won't be time after this," he said, acknowledging my disappointment with a pat on my back. I was upset to miss the game, but I felt worse for causing my friends to miss it.

We walked to an area where all the counselors waited. I felt like the amusement for the night. Everyone gathered around to watch the hot college-aged guy rescue the little girl from a demon. Jan was there too. She was maybe in her fifties, the only real adult in this crew. I knew her because she was the woman assigned to my cabin as our chaperone. Her presence was comforting, as she and I had gotten to know each other a little earlier that day.

The guy stood before me as the other counselors took Elise and our other friend aside. "Lindsey, will you come with me?" he asked.

"Can my friends come too?" I asked. I didn't want to leave them.

"They're going to stay right here, next to them," he said,

pointing at Jan and the rest of the twentysomethings. "They'll wait for you."

I looked at Elise, who was clearly growing uncomfortable. "Lindsey?" She said my name, unsure of what was going on. I cracked a smile for her and walked away with the guy.

The farther away we got from my friends, the more fearful I became. I wasn't necessarily afraid of the guy, but I was afraid of the demon. I didn't want to get hurt, and the movies made it seem like people who were possessed by demons got beat up until the demons left them. *I'm really scared*, I thought to myself. I heard my best friend cry out and call my name, and when I looked her way, a counselor pulled her in close for a hug. From the sound of her cries, you would've thought I was walking to my death. Our other friend stood there in shock, not saying a word—especially since she had once heard the voices too. I wondered if she was hoping she wouldn't be next.

He and I arrived at a random spot in the field, a football field away from my friends. He placed his hand on my shoulders and moved me a few steps away from him. Maybe it was the shadows on his face or how he was standing over me, but he seemed tall—and I felt very small.

He pulled out a tiny vial of water and opened the cap. I kept still. He struggled to get the cap off. *He looks nervous*, I thought. He began to sprinkle the little capsule of water on my head, while addressing the demon aggressively with his words. "Come out of her!" he yelled, over and over.

I stood there looking at him. He started to sweat—or maybe the water had sprinkled back on him as he shook the thing. The demon wasn't coming out, or at least I didn't feel it coming out. I stood still, head firmly in place—never once convulsing or violently throwing up like the possessed girl in the movie.

When the demon didn't budge, the guy grew frustrated. The look of fear in his eyes scared me. I could still hear Elise crying, and I could tell they were struggling to console her. I went in for a hug, afraid of the darkness around me, and the guy violently pushed me away. I stumbled a few steps back and began to cry myself. *I just want this to be over.*

And then, in an instant, it was all done. He pulled me in, finally, for a hug and tried to console me. But I was shaken. My body trembled in fear, my legs shaking the worst. The guy had a devious smile on his face, like he was proud of himself for having completed his first exorcism. He threw his arm around my shoulder in a way that professed his pride, and we walked back toward the others.

I wiped the tears from my eyes, trying to cover the shame of being the one who caused all of this. "You know," he said, "the demon in you spoke to me."

I looked up at him, quiet. *But I didn't hear anything!*

"He did," he said, giving the supposed demon a gender. "He said, 'I hate you!' But it was in your voice." I offered a gentle apology.

We finally reached the others, but I didn't have a chance to embrace my friends before being shoved into the middle of the circle of counselors with their hands raised and voices singing. I raised my hands with them, repeating over and over, "I love Jesus, I love Jesus." I was too afraid to say anything else.

I remember the moon and the way it provided me light that night. I was thankful for the way it lit up the space around me. I listened to the singing but felt separated from the worship. I spotted Jan and walked over to her, interrupting her spiritual experience by lightly tapping on her arm. She bent down to hear my question. "Why did this happen to me?" I asked. I still didn't understand.

She pitied me and took it upon herself to tell me the truth so this would never happen again. "Sweetie, do you doubt God? Because this is what happens when you do."

Doubt God? Am I the only one who struggles to believe God is real sometimes? Clearly, if anyone else doubted God, I had been the only one who admitted it. I didn't ask Jan any more questions. By the time the evening was over, I had nothing left in me—not even enough to play a game of flashlight tag. I was exhausted and now terrified of the dark.

I ran over to Elise and hugged her. I didn't want her to be afraid, so I said, "It's okay. It's out of me now"—fully believing that I had experienced my own deliverance that night.

Before bedtime, I grabbed my Bible and laid it next to my pillow. Jan agreed to let me and my friends put our mattresses in a dogpile on the floor because I was too afraid to sleep alone. It was warm inside our cabin, but I covered myself with a blanket anyway. I needed to feel the weight of protection over me. I hugged my Bible tightly to my chest, hoping it would be enough to scare the demon if he were to come back for me while I slept.

"That was a long night," I told Jen. "Every nighttime noise I heard made me think the demon was right there, hiding."

Jen rested her chin in her hand. She looked distressed, or just very frustrated by the situation.

"For the rest of the week, I observed the other kids," I told her. "I played in the swimming pool maybe once or twice and tried a pickup game of basketball. But I mostly just watched." Perhaps my soul was crushed, or maybe I was just humiliated. It was likely a little bit of both. But after that night, I developed anxiety about everything. I was afraid to mess up again, fearing I'd be thrown into hell by the God I had clearly upset.

The bus ride home was a lot quieter. The kids were exhausted from endless activities, but I was mostly tired from a mind that wouldn't rest. *God, I'm sorry I made you so mad. I didn't mean to. What do I have to do to fix it?* I took mental notes of what I could do to earn back God's approval. I knew I had some work to do.

Jen patiently waited for me to finish before she jumped in with her questions. "What happened after you got home? Did you tell your parents?"

"Yeah, I called them that night, actually. The counselors made me call them from the phone in the cafeteria after it happened."

"What did they say?"

"I don't remember. I don't think they said much of anything... but Jan forced me to call, and I was so nervous because I felt so embarrassed. I just blurted it right out as soon as they answered the phone. I said, 'Hey, I just want you to know that

I was possessed by a demon, but they got it out, okay?' I rushed the conversation. I didn't want my parents to be scared, so I didn't let on that it was anything to be afraid of."

"Lindsey," Jen spoke directly, "those counselors were wrong in what they did." She paused. I could tell she was struggling to wrap her head around the details. "And we're going to unpack this more, but you need to know that first."

I couldn't fully agree with her—that they were wrong. I didn't think I was possessed by a demon, but I also didn't think they were wrong to warn me about doubting God. And yet, I desperately wanted to believe otherwise. For a year after this camp experience, I lived in terror of demons. I was a paranoid child who read her Bible every day and prayed with other students at the flagpole before school started. After I shared what had happened with my middle school crush, the gossip broke and I got called "demon girl" at the lunch tables. The boys laughed at me and threw food at my table. But my best friend never left my side. She grew extremely protective of me, throwing the food back or yelling at them to shut up. She became the only constant friend I had—showing me care and attention that saved my life when I grew curious about suicide.

I let Jen work through her own emotions at hearing my story. I'd not yet witnessed her this visibly disturbed. I didn't say anything more, afraid to admit to her that the voices never actually went away, that I still doubted God, and that I feared I would never really be good enough. I lived right on the edge of hell, afraid one slip would send me into an eternity of suffering—without a God who cared to rescue me.

ten

Stained-Glass Sunday

After the church camp experience, my relationship with God was complicated. But it hadn't always been that way.

I wasn't raised by a family that went to church every Sunday, but I did know who God was from attending church with my grandparents on occasion. Additionally, I obsessed over the TV show *Touched by an Angel*, and watching this show was every bit of church to me as sitting in the back pew, crunching down on lollipops (which were supposed to keep us quiet) while listening to a reverend talk of things I could not understand.

I had a fascination with angels when I was a child. I was captivated at the thought that they were always around, protecting us. I loved to get lost in imagining how they'd swoop in at just the right time and save me from a scary situation. I'd lie in bed at night, stare at the glow-in-the-dark stars above my head, and think about how seriously fun it would be to fly.

I'd lace my fingers together and pray that God would make me a guardian angel when I grew up.

Then life became busy. Sports became our church, and the only TV I watched was Friday night TGIF shows.

Later, when I moved to Tennessee, I felt like a foreigner around all the religious talk. People used lingo I'd never heard before. They'd ask me questions like, "What's your story?" And I'd reply, "What story are you talking about?" Or they'd ask, "When did you become a Christian?" And I'd think, *I'm not even sure. I think I'm still becoming one.*

Jesus was a distant character in a story that made sense to me only through stained-glass windows in an old Presbyterian church. The sun would shine through the windows and tell a colorful story of a kind-eyed man named Jesus. There, I concluded, as I settled my gaze on the curious children sitting around him, that Jesus was probably a pretty cool friend—a person I'd want to sit next to if I could transport myself into the image in those windows. Then, there was the wooden cross that made me sad. When I looked at it, I was reminded that this same Jesus man was nailed to it—all to "save me from death." I didn't quite understand how a man way back then could save me from death, but I didn't ask questions as a child.

At the same time, I was attuned to a darkness that always felt close by. I felt hunted. Maybe it was the result of the scary movies I watched or the number of times I played the board games where we tried to access the spiritual realm. Or it could have been from the first moment I encountered death—when my Little League softball teammate's three-year-old sister ran into the road to catch a firefly and was hit by a car. Though young, I noticed the grief of this family and watched the sadness overtake them.

A death can bring you to your knees with big, hard questions, no matter how young you are. I witnessed an imperfect world unfolding right before my eyes. So, if you were to ask me when I first became a Christian, I would tell you it was the night I shut my bedroom door as a young child, sat in front of a small, lit Christmas tree, and prayed for the very first time—for little Samantha to fly free like the angels in heaven and for her family to not be so sad anymore.

As a child, my spirituality was free and innocent. My imagination ran wild, and I found God in lightning bugs and baseball as much as I found Jesus in stained-glass windows and lollipops. God wasn't only pursuing me through beauty; he was pursuing me in sadness too—knowing as I got older I'd need the One to call on amid grief.

I really loved those Sunday mornings though.

I grabbed my sweater and ran out the door. My grandpa was picking me up for church, and we still had to stop and get my nana (his mother). I rushed, knowing Papaw liked to get to church early. I loved every moment I spent with him, and going early with him meant I could play the church handbells before the rest of our family joined us. A quartet of gospel voices filled the car as he played his music loudly over the speakers. I'd listen to him sing and watch his hands keep the beat on the steering wheel. It was like being invited into my grandfather's sacred world. I tried to learn the lyrics so I could sing along.

As we pulled into Nana's driveway, the garage door slowly lifted up. There she was, as if we'd timed it perfectly. She wore a beautiful, colorful dress and with a sweater draped over her arms. I couldn't help but notice her feet trapped inside her pantyhose as they poked out from the open toes of her sandals. Her glasses were edgy, both in style and in physicality, with sharp corners on the outside points. Papaw helped her into the back seat, and she sat next to me. She was a poised woman. My favorite memory of her was the day she and her sister, whom we called our Aunt Mary, taught me how to play the card game slapjack. I slapped Mary's hand so hard they both broke out in laughter. Even if I don't remember many words Nana said, I remember loving her presence. I didn't always get to ride with Papaw to church—just on the luckiest days.

As we pulled up to First Presbyterian Church, the glow of colors coming from the stained-glass windows could be seen from the parking lot. Bold blue skies and deep green hills, the red of Moses's coat as he held the stone tablet of commandments—all of them inviting me to come in and see. My favorite window was on the north side of the sanctuary: a brilliant angel with large golden wings, dressed in white, raising his hands to heaven. Just below the angel was Jesus, who knelt beside a rock, wearing a red garment with white sleeves. His face was turned upward as a beam of light shone down from heaven onto his adoring face. And I thought to myself, *Ah, so that's what angels look like!*

My parents, who had just arrived, made their way to our usual spot—up two flights of stairs to the very top row, middle section; we had the best view up there. My sister and I rushed to the table where the church volunteers laid out goodie bags of crossword puzzles and candy to keep the kids entertained during the sermon. We each grabbed one and sifted through the bags before finding our seats with our parents.

The pews were lined with red, fuzzy fabric. If you slid your hand one direction, it was velvety smooth to touch. But if you sat down in a dress and pantyhose, you stuck to the fabric like Velcro.

Church began with a handbell choir. They'd play a song or two, and we kids would listen with suckers in our mouths as my parents opened up the white program to study the itinerary of the morning. My eyes focused in on a large wooden cross that hung in the front of the church, high above the choir. From our bird's-eye view—the top pew, back row, of First Presbyterian Church—I was at eye level with Jesus.

The simple wooden cross awed me, even at such a young age.

Rays of sunlight penetrated the stained-glass windows, and the image of children sitting around the feet of Jesus lit up the room. This old church building, founded in 1851, resounded with beauty.

After handbells and opening prayers, the reverend called for the children to come up to the front and sit as he taught us our very own lesson on the love of Jesus. My sister and I raced down the stairs, each heel step clicking. We joined the crowd of children up front and took our place on the steps before the congregation. The reverend's wife handed us the microphone to share our own interpretations on the story of love, and the adults oohed and aahed as our young voices echoed through the sanctuary.

After the story was finished, we were directed back to our seats. Then we demonstrated our best fast walk toward our parents. I wanted to be the first back up the stairs, always feeling the need to make it a competition. Then I found my goodie bag and colored until the sermon was over.

The closing of church was a prayer in unison, followed by the benediction sung over us by the reverend.

The Lord bless you and keep you.

The Lord make his face to shine upon you.

And give you peace. Amen.

He'd cue the organ, which was our cue that church was over. When the crowd erupted in conversation and handshakes, I knew it was time to go find my grandparents up toward the front. I smiled and said hello as my grandma and grandpa proudly introduced me and my siblings to their friends. I knew what was coming next: silver dollar pancakes and a large glass of orange juice. We always went to the local pancake spot after church. My grandparents treated us.

There was something special about that church—something alive within the atmosphere that stayed close beside me like a friend. Like a warm, gentle presence of the spirit. I felt safe there. The stained-glass windows, the handbells and church choir, the wooden cross that drew my curious mind to stillness and reverence, the goodie bags of candy and coloring pages, the handshakes and familiar faces—all of it left a mark of security on my heart that lasted beyond the years we attended church there.

Long after we stopped going to church regularly, I still thought about the phrase that was spoken over us time and time again. *Jesus hung on a cross for me. He died—for me.* After being tucked into bed at night, I'd think about this man Jesus. Who was he, really? And why did he have to die for me?

"Wow, Linds." The way Jen shortened my name reminded me of my grandpa. He'd been the first one in my family to call me that. He had also recently passed away, and I missed him a lot.

"That sounds like a beautiful church experience," Jen continued. "And I'm so happy you have the memory to hold onto."

It was beautiful, and it was the memory I returned to when I tried to wrap my mind around the church camp exorcism. How could God have hated me *so* much? That night at church camp shaped my faith in a horrific way, tainting the innocence of my honest talks with Jesus. But the whole experience never really added up to the earliest truth I'd learned about God: that he welcomes our doubt, and his love never leaves us. I have First Presbyterian Church to thank for that.

eleven

The Spiral

Ink fell onto paper with each stroke of a heavy pen, weighted with secrets begging to be let loose.

I'm going to have to tell her.

I read and reread those loaded words, weighing my present anxiety against the possibility that just one sentence, spoken out loud, had the power to set me free.

Just a few days earlier, Jen had reached over, grabbed a book off her side table, and handed it to me. . . .

"It's a journal," she said nonchalantly. "It's for you to write it all down in."

"Write *what* all down in?"

"All of those swirling thoughts in your head." She smiled. "I've watched you circling through them. I know when you're processing. I can see it on your face."

I am a deep thinker, I thought.

I rubbed my hand over the cover of the book, eyeing the

texture as I traced the pale pink and yellow design with my fingers.

"I've never been one to keep a diary." I almost laughed in embarrassment at the thought of writing my feelings down. That practice was too sensitive for a personality like mine. *Diaries are for girly girls,* I heard my mind say. *And I am not that.*

I had kept my eyes lowered on the book, not knowing how to receive the gift. I wondered if I'd even be able to put words to the thoughts that were spinning all so fast, first in my heart and then in my head.

Is it possible to think myself into a different story—one that is easier?

I placed the book down on the floor next to me. I could feel the nudging of a story ready to unfold. Pages torn. Binding worn. A story of fury and passion, and heavy amounts of self-doubt and despair. An unraveling. Maybe, though, in the end, it would be a story of hope.

There was nothing special about this journal yet, but what it could become was thrilling. This journal wasn't a holy book itself, but the makings of a book about a holy life—a holy surrender. About an anxious heart searching for freedom.

Later that night, I sat on my bed and opened my journal. I read those words again: *I'm going to have to tell her.* My fear of coming out already showed through the angsty, scribbled words and run-on sentences that now filled that book. I picked up my pen and continued writing.

I am stuck inside the walls of those words and what they

mean. I've been comfortable to stay right here in the middle of the slow-building pressure, knowing there was no need to run forward or turn around and go back, but now the walls are closing in on me. I have to decide which way I'll go. My marriage is the path ahead, or I could run back to what I've known and lose everything I've built so far. But not making a decision will crush me.

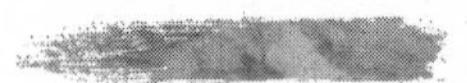

I parked my car and rushed up the sidewalk to Jen's front door. I apologized for being late as she opened the front door to invite me in.

"This is the first time you've ever been late. I think you're allowed one." She was playful, but I was frustrated by my tardiness.

We sat down and both let out deep, heavy breaths. "So." She paused, letting me get settled in. "How are you today?"

"That's a loaded question."

I flashed back to earlier that morning. To the yelling. I still felt the sting in my knuckles from putting my fist through our bedroom wall.

"This morning was hard." I downplayed the difficulty, knowing it would take some gradual uncovering before I could be completely vulnerable. "I'm doing all right, I guess."

She looked at me with a *tell me more* look.

"I'm just tired. I don't know how much longer I can do this."

"Do what?" she prompted.

"Stay married."

I was gaining ground in processing the hurts of my childhood, but so many unresolved questions still circled around my marriage—such as, How could we keep fighting for our survival when I wasn't seeking intimacy with him? This new lack of desire confused me because we struggled to keep our hands off each other before we were married.

I was weary and wanted permission to give up—though I would not get it from Jen. She was empathetic, but she was no quitter.

"Our marriage has been hard from the beginning."

"How so?"

I'm going to have to tell her.

"I am the reason why my marriage is so difficult. . . . I made everything fall apart."

"Hmm . . ." A look of doubt crossed her face. "What makes you say that?"

"What I haven't told you yet is that I'm also attracted to women—and before I was married, I was in a relationship with another woman."

Well, that was easier than I thought it would be!

The words continued to pour out the moment I opened my mouth.

"I felt so alive with her. It ended abruptly. But I never really shared with Jonathan what she meant to me, so it came as a shock when I told him the truth one week after our honeymoon. We were fighting about something . . ." I took a minute to try remembering what started it, but to no avail. "To be honest, I don't even remember what the fight was over, but I was feeling so confused at *everything*—why we just kept fighting, why our marriage was so unexciting once the wedding was over. I guess the reality was starting to set in—that I had promised the rest of my life to this man, and I don't think I really understood what I was gaining. It felt more like a loss . . . and then I just told him. I said, 'I can't do this anymore. I think I'm gay.'"

The lack of judgment on Jen's face was comforting, so I continued processing with her.

"I crushed him. I just kept telling him I was sorry, over and over."

The memory was still fresh: how he reached his hands over and gently touched mine. I was so sorry to have played with the heart of the only man who'd ever truly loved me, cared for me, protected me. I remembered how sad his eyes were, but at the same time, I saw a hint of relief in them, as though he'd sensed something bigger going on.

Jen was still with me.

"That was when he first pleaded for me to get help. I haven't really told you everything yet . . ."

"Well," she reassured, "maybe it wasn't time for all of it until now. But things are making a little more sense to me as to why you feel so trapped in this marriage."

"A part of my heart died the day we got married. It just took me a few days to really feel the impact of it."

"How so?"

"All the fantasy of an easy, happy marriage vanished on

our honeymoon. I just knew it would be hard. There was no way around it. I couldn't see any path forward, together . . . because I had no solution to the problem I was really facing."

I continued. "I want a life with him, but my heart is attached to someone else—some*place* else. It feels like another lifetime."

"Is she still in the picture?"

I shook my head.

"What happened?"

"I just walked away from her, told her it was done, and then I got engaged shortly after."

I moved my hand up to my chest, like I was nursing an ache in my heart. The pain of the loss was still very present.

"Ah, so you were seeing her while you were seeing your husband . . ." She was putting two and two together. "Did you allow yourself to grieve the loss?"

"It is not worth grieving . . ."

"And why is that?"

I couldn't give a good answer. *Because homosexuality is wrong?* I wasn't sure I believed that, but it felt like the answer I'd convinced myself of. But grief shows no partiality. Even if I couldn't justify a reason to grieve, the loss of something significant triggers pain—and I felt a deep, debilitating pain in her absence. Our relationship *was*, at least, worthy of an actual goodbye.

"You said your husband asked you get help, so where did you go?"

"I didn't know where to go, so I drove to the church."

I brushed the tears off my face. The thought of never knowing what she and I could have become was what hurt the most.

"What about her do you miss so much?"

"Feeling safe and feeling so alive. I miss her affection."

I realized in that moment that *me missing her* wasn't just about this one woman. It was an identity—an entire empire I'd built around my heart. In this empire I'd felt most seen, most alive, most cared for and nurtured—feelings I didn't find naturally in my relationship with my husband. Or with any man, for that matter.

"Do you believe it's possible to feel those things within your marriage now?"

Jen was asking good questions, but I could not give sure answers.

"What I know is that I've made a promise to my husband, and I believe I was clearheaded on that day in December when I said 'I do.' So, I'd like to not give up just yet."

"I hope you'll hear me on this, Lindsey," Jen said with conviction. "To be loved, and to love someone yourself, and to desire affection—none of these things are wrong." I replayed the message in my head again: *my desire to be loved is not wrong.* "I believe you can find this within your marriage . . . but"—she paused—"it's going to take work."

"I don't know where to start."

"Maybe you actually do," she offered.

And once she said that, I did. I knew right away.

It starts with grief.

twelve

A Radiant Woman

I got on my knees and began to pray. I wasn't sure if God would hear me, but I knew I'd never be heard if I stayed quiet. I felt a little silly. *What do I even say?* I lowered my head into my arms to cancel out the light; I struggled to focus. *Just a few minutes with you is all I'm asking for.* I fidgeted, moving from my knees to a more comfortable seat. I stilled my mind and told the distractions that they'd have to wait. My thoughts slowed down. Even if I quit right now, it was more time than I'd given God before.

I felt pressed to stay in the tension of this moment as I attempted to access God. Then something occurred to me: *Is he waiting to be invited?* Any well-mannered guest would not come barging in through the front door. Even when they know you well, they'll usually give a light knock to let you know they've arrived. I felt the knock. Something in my heart, lightly tapping.

May I come in?

I humored myself with a little role-play, but if I wanted to do this, I'd need to use my voice and not just my mind.

"God, you can come in now," I spoke quietly. I wasn't sure I could handle this much of my own vulnerability, even when no one else was around. I continued praying with my eyes closed. If I opened them, the distractions would reappear. I placed my hands over my eyes and rested my elbows on my knees. An image began to form in my mind, almost like a dream. There, I saw a woman holding a girl in her arms. I asked God, "What is this dream I'm having?" I heard nothing, but I kept watching . . .

I glanced to the sky and saw the dark clouds rolling in. A storm was brewing; the rain would come soon. The thunder rumbled, and an electric current ran wildly through the atmosphere. The force was magnetic, drawing me in. I looked at my palms and could feel the energy running through to the ends of my fingertips. I stood before a building, at the foot of its steps—steps that would lead me to the next mission: the rescue of the one trapped inside. With each step up, the rain began to fall. The closer I got, the more magnetic the draw. I reached a wooden door that was as tall as it was thick, about three persons. Then lightning struck, and a blast of sound penetrated the doorway in front of me. I fell to the ground and lost consciousness.

Loud shouts came from within the walls. I couldn't hear or see what was really happening but listened closely as I tried to make out what was being said. My body trembled. The concrete underneath me felt cold as ice, and I wished for a blanket. My eyes opened slightly, and I found myself on the floor of a room with dark hues and ripped furniture. How I got from the outside steps into a room with no windows I could not explain. The shouts were hostile, and they closed in around me. All at once, the door to my room was blown down with a high-powered wind. A wave of heat ushered in and soothed the aches of my bones. A crackling fire was before me, creeping its way closer and closer—like it was spreading toward me along the ground. What I noticed behind the flame was a radiant woman, unlike anyone I've seen before, who called out a deep reverence in me. Her flame stopped right before me. She did not walk before the flame or after it, but rather inside of it. Yet she was not burned. She knelt before me and matched my curiosity with her own eagerness. The look on her face was gentle—mothering, even. I felt the warmth of her flame come underneath me, sweeping me up into her presence. Her comforting heat pressed against my face as I drifted back to sleep.

The rain poured hard. The lightning cracked, and I awoke again on the steps.

"Get up! You must go in and reach her." I looked around and saw no one.

"Hello? Who are you speaking to?"

The mysterious voice spoke again. "She is up the stairs

behind the first door. Kick it down. You'll see her asleep. Lift her up gently. You *must* be gentle. Carry her down the stairs and out the door."

I regained full consciousness, although for a moment I was certain I was still dreaming. I did not search for the physical body of this voice; I sensed it belonged to no human being but one of a spirit. A holy one. One who would show himself if he wanted to. Still, his words were empowering, like a dose of courage I'd never known.

"Do not be fearful of their threats," he continued. "Do not even look them in the eye; they cannot harm you. Hurry. Up the stairs!"

I ran through the door, and my pace quickened as I skipped every second step. Time was pressing, yet I was surprisingly unafraid we'd run out of it. I reached the first door and shook the handle. It was locked.

"Kick it down." His voice spoke as clear as if he were standing right beside me. I looked at my small feet and back up at the door. "Kick it down!"

I raised my foot and thrust it right above the handle. The door fell, and there she was. I could not contain my emotion. I wept as I saw her small frame lying on the concrete. The faintest sign of life rose in her chest. I knew I could not leave her here another moment. "Grab her and leave. Now is the time."

I stepped carefully toward the woman who lay before me. I gazed at her with an eagerness. There was curiosity behind her eyes, but I could also see a grave hopelessness. With every inch of will in me, I bent down and lifted her into my arms.

I knew what to do next; the mission was clear before me: *get out*. I held her close to my chest and she drifted back to sleep. Two steps out, and the shouts of threats began.

"Give her to me!" the first man said.

"She does not belong to you. She will come back to me!" a second man shouted.

"You are wasting your time with this one," a third man scoffed.

"If you leave this place, I will kill you both!" the second man shouted, as if he owned the rights to her.

The threats heightened, but I remained focused, still cradling her body in my arms. I remembered what the Spirit said when it gave me this mission: "Do not be fearful of their threats. They cannot harm you." I moved with the fearlessness of a raging fire, ready to burn whoever came close to her. As I neared the front door, the shouts lost their power, and out I stepped.

I looked above me and noticed I was standing beneath a shelter of tall tulip trees. They were all around me. Trunks so thick I wondered how many hundreds of years ago they were first planted. All I saw above me, and beside me, was a deep, rejuvenating green—and I realized in that moment I was *hidden* inside this forest of trees. I stood there, questioning why this was the next spot the Spirit chose to take us to. Not that I didn't love the serenity, but now I was outside the action of the mansion that held captive all the soul-shattered women, desperate for their own deliverance. Where was the young woman I'd held in my arms? I was now only looking on from a distance as the front door to this place was several steps away from me.

"Why are we here?" I asked. I felt him throw his arm around me to pull me in.

"Look there." He pointed toward the door. "Any minute now you will see her walk out," he said.

"But who? Who will walk out?" I directed my eyes toward the entrance of the house and could hear shouts coming from within the walls.

"Any minute," I heard him whisper.

I held my eyes on the large wooden door. Quiet with anticipation. Suddenly, the door burst open, and he was right. There she was. A radiant woman: an ember full of flame.

"Ah-ha!" His arms jolted into the air like the mission was finished. "There she is! Look at her. Wow."

His voice became shaky, as though this moment was so thrilling it took his breath away. I could hear the passion in his voice, but the unspoken delight in his eyes drew me in. Who was this woman he was so drawn to, so captivated by her beauty? I turned my eyes back to the woman. She marched down the stairs with fire in her bones; nothing could stop her. She held tightly to the young woman in her arms, hugging her to her chest as if the weight of her lifeless body was of no burden at all.

As she approached us, I noticed a familiarity with this girl she carried. "Who is she?" I asked, not taking my eyes off her. He knew which of the women I was referring to. Turning my gaze toward him, I was caught by surprise that he was staring solely at me. I had suddenly drawn his attention.

"There is something peculiar about this young woman she holds. Strange. Like I know her from somewhere."

He turned his eyes back toward the woman in flame, and I focused on her too. I noticed the look on her face. It was the same look of compassion—and sheer eagerness—I watched her give the near lifeless young woman, cold on the concrete floor.

I felt the heat of the woman draw near as she headed straight for us. I revered her power, but I was unafraid. She stopped right in front of me. In that moment, almost instinctively, I knew that I was to reach out and take the one whom she was holding. I opened my arms as she laid the body in my embrace. The young woman, once lifeless, now covered in her own flame.

The Spirit pulled me closer. "That woman . . . is you."

My eyes shot open. This dream was far too real. I fumbled for a pen in the drawer of Jonathan's work desk and grabbed my journal. *I have to write this down before I forget.* I penned every detail I could remember. I wasn't just the lifeless woman who was nearly dead in her shame; I was also the woman whose silhouette was covered in fire and flame. This dream energized me, and I gained a renewed sense of urgency—as if a real woman's life hung in the balance. I knew this: I was the only one fit to rescue her.

thirteen

Dangerous Fantasy

My foot tapped the floor beneath me. I was struggling to conceal my nervousness. Jen was eager to dig deeper, as was I, but I knew with the digging came the uncovering, and I was at the mercy of whatever was revealed.

"So, tell me more about your relationships with women."

"They are . . . complicated." I paused. "Can I talk about my distaste for men instead?" I laughed. That subject would at least get us started. I was being playful, but I was also being truthful; I'd been burned one too many times.

I lived on the edge of anxiety, always present, wondering if I'd be the next victim of a violent, lustful man whom I couldn't outfight. As such, I was never fully at ease around men.

With women, though—*deep sigh*—it was different. Women are gentle. Women are beautiful. Women are trustworthy. Women are good listeners and good protectors. What I longed for was to be held, protectively, in the arms of a woman who would not unwrap me until the world felt safe again.

Some friendships had been more difficult to navigate than others. I was easily codependent, and I owned it. I'd lost two friendships because of it, and losing those relationships had been nothing short of grievous, both times. I hated losing friends—whether by literal death or the loss of relationship. It pained me either way. I had gotten so used to sadness that sometimes I wondered if I was more friendly with grief than I was with joy.

I love loving, and I love being loved. But through years of building a life "worthy" of approval and forming unhealthy habits as a way of earning acceptance, my desire to be wanted became an addiction—and that addiction stole the person from me every single time. Like most who struggle with addiction, I couldn't strong-arm this. I had to see it for what it was, own it, and call it by its name: *love addict.*

"When I got married, I lost my hiding place." I took in a deep breath. "There was one woman I had started a relationship with and wasn't quite ready to leave. But I did, and right after I got married, she was the one I thought of often."

"Tell me about her," Jen nudged.

She enticed me with her charm. Her dark brown eyes penetrated my loneliness like the tip of a spear. She could see in, and she wanted in. Words of fantasy left her mouth like a melody off her lips, and I was attracted to the song. Her attention soothed my aches—a long-awaited comfort. She whispered secrets to me, and I entertained them. The darkness of lust swirled around space, tangling us up in the ties that bound us. *How far could this go?*

I'd just moved to Tennessee, shaking the Indiana dust from my feet. I had an interview at a new salon that opened up right next to Vanderbilt's campus. I dressed myself to play the part: black slacks and a black blazer, with a low-cut, light pink shirt and black heels. This style felt unfamiliar compared to my typical choice of jeans and a hooded sweatshirt.

I parked my flashy, burnt orange, two-door sports car up the block, and on my walk to the salon, I took time to breathe in the new city, new friends, and a potential new job. I passed by a music venue that had confiscated my fake ID just a few nights earlier. The security guard knew at first glance that the picture wasn't me and said, "If you just show me your real ID, I'll let you in." You only had to be eighteen to get in, but I was too prideful. I scoffed at him for not believing it was me, then turned around and left. My friends wondered why I didn't just do what he asked so I could get in. *Because I'm too damn prideful*, I thought.

As I got closer to the entrance of the salon, I could smell the fragrance coming from inside the building. The smell was alluring, a sharp contrast to the smell coming from the sewage plate I had to step over to get inside.

I pushed my way through the door and was greeted by the girl who worked the front desk. The music gave the space a good vibe, but it was hard to hear over the sound of multiple hairdryers blowing at the same time.

"Are you Lindsey?" I heard a woman say as she walked over to introduce herself.

"Hey! Yes, I am," I said, sticking my hand out to initiate the formal introduction.

"It's nice to meet you," she said. "I'm Jade." She waved me over closer to her. "You can follow me back to my office."

It didn't take long to feel a connection to her personality. I'm guessing she felt attracted to mine, too, because I was hired on the spot. I started the following day.

Jade was outgoing. Very fun and flirty with every client that came in for their appointment. She made sure to introduce me to them, but it was never just my name they got. She'd add in things like: "This is Lindsey. Isn't she beautiful?" And they'd answer, "Yes!"—which, of course they would, because it would be rude to ignore her or disagree. Or, with a glance my way, she'd say, "Meet Lindsey. She's our newest girl, and we're really happy she's here." I didn't mind her flirtatious attention, but it was never subtle. I wondered if she intended it to be that way.

Jade was good at sales and making her clients feel like they belonged with us. She was eager to train me as I got promoted to the head concierge at the front desk. I had my license in cosmetology, but this new role had more perks. I was paid more and did less work than the stylists did. I just needed to make sure our clients were happy, so I did just that by flattering them in my own way.

This new role also meant taking the closing shift—just me, Jade, and Jade's business partner, Lex. I was sweeping the floors on my first night when they both approached me. "Lex," Jade said, "meet Lindsey. Lindsey, meet Lex." I smiled and said hi. "Lex is not just my business partner, but also my *life* partner." Jade emphasized the word *life*, making sure I knew what that meant. She studied my body language. "Is this going to be a problem for you?"

The notion didn't move me in any way. I had my own secrets that made me more familiar with her world than she knew. "No, not at all," I said with a smile.

"Good," she said, as I continued sweeping the floors.

I found stability in my new routine. Every afternoon I'd come in for my closing shift. I parked my car up the street, walked a block downhill, passed by the bar, and covered my nose as I stepped over the sewage plate to enter the salon. The compliments and playful run-ins with Jade continued, and I welcomed her attention.

It was a late evening, with clients still receiving services well past eight o'clock. Closing the salon down would mean an even longer night. Jade came over and said, "Lex and I are going to order some takeout. You want to eat with us?"

I wouldn't turn down a free meal *or* a chance to hang out with them past regular business hours. "Yeah, I'd like that." I admired how she just took care of things. If it were up to me, I wouldn't think about dinner until after I had gotten home and was starving. I'd typically look into the fridge, realize I still hadn't gone grocery shopping, make myself a peanut butter and jelly sandwich, and call it a night.

Jade sent Lex to pick up the food, leaving Jade and me to finish up the cleaning after the last client. She brought out a bottle of wine. "You want some?"

I looked at the bottle, feeling conflicted because I hadn't had a single sip of alcohol since leaving Indiana and moving to Tennessee. "Sure, I'll take a glass." She screwed in the wine opener and pulled out the cork. She took a stemless wineglass down from the cabinet above the sink and poured me a glass. She handed it to me, making sure to touch my hand as she did. My heart pulsed, and we took our first sips together. Her lips parted like she was about to say something, but then she closed them. I looked at her with curious eyes. *She is playing mind games*, I thought. She took another sip.

"So, Lindsey . . ." She moved just slightly closer to me. *She's definitely playing mind games.* "Have you ever kissed a girl?" She asked the question quietly, like it was something to be quiet about. But no one else was in the salon—just her and me. I took a longer sip of my wine, implying that I had. "You have!" Her eyes widened. "Did you like it?"

Why is she asking me this? I wondered what she was up to, but I wasn't put off by it. "I did," I replied.

Lex walked in with a large plastic bag of expensive Italian food from a restaurant down the street. "That took forever!" she said as she placed the food on the countertop next to us. She eyed Jade first, and then me.

Jade said, "We were just pouring some wine. I'll get you a glass." I stepped back and allowed them to sort through the food. I grabbed a few chairs and circled them around a small side table one of the stylists used. We could eat out of our to-go containers, but we would need a table to put the wine on. Jade handed me my food, and the women joined me in the chairs.

"I like the three of us hanging out," Jade mentioned. "Lex, Lindsey told me she's kissed a girl before."

Lex was taking a bite of her food but finished swallowing before showing her excitement. "What! Then, clearly, you're a lesbian." We all laughed. Though something told me she wasn't really joking, I wondered if she was right.

As the night went on, we opened more bottles of wine. After talking about some of the things we had talked about, I wondered if I was still being faithful to my boyfriend. Regardless, I wasn't thinking too much about him at the moment. For all he knew, I was working late—not sitting with my lesbian bosses drinking wine. I made sure to stop after three glasses, knowing I would need to drive myself home. But I should have stopped before that. I'd forgotten how much a tolerance is built up, and after not drinking for months, I discovered that my tolerance was low.

Jade and Lex took turns showing me special attention. I started to feel caught up in a game of cat and mouse, where I was the mouse and they were the two cats. Whoever charmed me first would catch the bait.

Jen interrupted me, causing me to feel embarrassed, as if I'd shared too much. "How long did you keep this from Jonathan?"

"I didn't lie to him about their flirtation with me or the fact that they were lesbians, but I never told him that I loved their attention. I actively participated in the game." I felt guilty for misleading Jonathan like I did. I could have spared us a lot of pain if I'd just let him know I was questioning my sexuality.

"How long did you keep working there?"

"Not long. Trying to balance two separate lives is harder than it looks." Jen nodded in agreement—not as if she knew from experience, but as if she knew the truth that the deeper you hide in something the harder it is to get out of it.

Before long, Jade and I were rubbing shoulders whenever we would pass each other at work and holding hands beneath the table when we'd leave after-hours and find a local spot for a drink. I fell heavily under the influence of her intoxicating charm. It was only a matter of time before our two worlds would collide and Jonathan would show up to my work one evening. On the night he finally did, I was surprised to see him walk through the front doors—as if he'd caught me in a life I didn't want to share with him.

"Oh my gosh, hey!" I said as I ran over to give him a hug. He kissed me on my forehead, and I immediately felt a boulder of guilt in my stomach. Jade walked out of her office and introduced herself to Jonathan, looking at me and affirming him. "He's cute, Lindsey!" *Yeah, he's very cute and gentle and loyal, and I'm going to ruin all of it.*

He smiled and focused his attention back on me. "I just wanted to stop in and say hi. You gonna be home on time tonight?" he asked politely. I locked eyes with him and wanted nothing more than to confess my budding relationship with her. Tell him I was sorry. I didn't want to admit that I'd been cheating on him. I wished he could just see it in my eyes. "Yeah, I will . . ."

The salon was closing, and I had every intention to leave on time. Then Jade came around the corner with a new bottle of wine, already opened, waving it back and forth, offering it to me without exchanging any words.

I can't tonight. I need to go home. I want to be with Jonathan.

"You know I'll take some!"

Damnit. Why did I say that? Why is it so hard for me to deny her?

I knew it was Jonathan I wanted to go home to. I couldn't picture taking Jade home to meet my family or growing old with her or buying our first dog together. (Did she even like dogs?) Whatever this was between her and me was pure fantasy: a life that wasn't real. Sure, our feelings were real, but we were high on infatuation and alcohol. My future with her paled in comparison to the man I'd committed to when he asked me to be his girlfriend. The man who'd soon ask me to marry him.

"Come dance with us," Lex said as she took my hand and pulled me up from my seat. Jade switched the playlist in the salon and turned it up. *Where's my alcohol?* I grabbed the bottle of wine, forgetting about the glass. As we danced, I got more and more drunk, and the girls got more and more jealous for my attention. When Jade went to the restroom, Lex grabbed my hand. She pulled me into the kitchen, but she didn't have to drag me; I went willingly, curious where she was taking me.

She smiled nervously. "Do you want me too?" I can only imagine she was catching on to my and Jade's attraction to each other. I turned my head toward the ground and smiled, hoping I could hide that my answer was a no. I didn't want to hurt her feelings. She moved in closer and nudged me into the back wall. She was very close, and I knew what was coming next: she kissed me.

I panicked. *Oh God, this is not what I want.* I was also somewhat annoyed; if I was going to kiss anyone and then have to fess up to my boyfriend, I would have rather it have been Jade. I kissed Lex back but gently pushed her away. "Lex, I can't do this." She backed up and lowered her eyes. I could tell she felt so unwanted. "It's just that I have a boyfriend and I really love him." I took her hand. "It's okay though. I'm not mad about this, okay?"

Truth was, I *wasn't* mad about it. She did what any normal person would do when they felt a mutual connection in the heat of a moment. I walked out of the room; it was time for me to go home. Jade was at the front of the salon popping open a new bottle of wine when I walked up to her. "I have to go home, okay?" I knew as I walked out of the salon that night that it would be the last night I worked there.

I woke up the following morning with sobering clarity.

I called Jonathan. "Hey, I will explain everything later, but I'm quitting my job today." He was quiet as I gave him a few details, but I figured he might have an idea why based on my not coming to see him after work. *He probably thinks I'm just getting uncomfortable with the flirting.* I wasn't. I was just afraid that if I told the truth, I'd lose him.

I knew the decision to quit was what was best for me, but it was a hard decision to make, and saying goodbye to Jade wasn't the hardest part. This other life made me feel so alive. The closer I got to the salon, the tighter the knot in my stomach grew.

I parked my car up the street, walked a block downhill, and passed by the bar for the last time. I didn't hang up my coat but walked straight into Jade's office where she was sitting doing paperwork. "Hey," I said, closing the door behind me. *Does she know that Lex kissed me last night?*

"Hi," she said, flirty and clearly oblivious. She stopped what she was doing and focused her attention on me, smiling. I studied her eyes, knowing this was likely the last time I'd see her. I looked at her pretty face and her pretty hair and her adorable small-framed body that easily fit inside my arms. "I need to quit." The words tumbled out awkwardly.

She was still. Then she stiffened up, straightened her suit jacket, and stood to her feet without saying a word.

I stuttered through an "I'm sorry," knowing I had disappointed her. I could give her no real reason why I needed to leave, and she was angry about it. When she asked me why, I just gave her a look of regret. I was so sorry to do this to her.

What was I to say anyway? That we'd gone too far? That

I couldn't see a future with us, so I needed to quit being her employee? That Lex kissed me? That I'd come to the conclusion that neither of us could give each other the love we sought?

Lex entered the office and said hello to me before noticing things weren't good. Jade walked right past her and slammed the door shut. I looked at Lex and said, "I'm sorry, Lex, but I have to quit."

She sat down in Jade's chair. "Is this about last night?" she asked, and I could tell she felt bad.

"No, no, it's not. I have no regrets, okay? I just have to leave." Lex was gentler in her response. I felt like she would miss me, but I didn't doubt she was ready to have her girlfriend's whole attention back. "I understand."

"Jade is so mad," I said.

"Yeah, but she'll be okay," Lex reassured me. She was ready to take on the responsibility of consoling her. I walked out of the office and stopped just before exiting the front door. I watched Jade aggressively folding towels, showing no emotion, like she couldn't have cared less to see me go. My heart sank in my chest. *See ya, Jade.* I walked out.

As I walked up the hill to my car, I couldn't stop the tears from coming. When I got inside, I let out a loud sob. This ending didn't feel good. I called Jonathan and told him it was done and I'd be right over.

I stopped by the gas station to buy a pack of cigarettes first. It had been years since I last smoked, but it was a way I knew how to calm down. I gave one knock before letting myself into the house Jonathan shared with three other guys. He moved aside as I barged in and collapsed on his couch. My clothes reeked of cigarettes. He asked, "Are you okay?"

I'm not okay . . . not even the least bit. But I'm with you now, I thought. *You'll replace the feelings I have for her. You're who I want anyway. I just need to give it some time.*

"Yeah, I feel great," I lied.

"I didn't know then how much I'd miss her." I looked at Jen, hoping she was still with me. "I just . . . ran away." I was still feeling the loss. "Sure, I wanted Jonathan, but I felt so alive . . . and I miss feeling alive."

Retelling the story reopened the wound. *This is why I'm here*, I reminded myself, *sitting in front of this woman. I'm so lost.*

Jen looked at me in the quiet, allowing me to sit in the sadness before she said anything more. She must have gathered that the more I talked about Jade the more I missed her.

"I just wish I wouldn't have run away." I still felt regret for not just being honest with her.

"So, what happened after you first told Jonathan you might be gay?"

"It was a horrible fight. But I went looking for help." I was still confused about how to move through all of this. "The thing is, nothing has really changed. We are still in the thick of it."

fourteen

A Pull to Stay

My thoughts went back to the day I had thrown my ring at Jonathan. To the time he begged me to get help, just one week after returning home from our honeymoon. The moment I walked directly into the church building and blurted out, "I need help." Those were the only words I could gather as the woman greeted me at the front door. She hooked her arm in mine and walked me to the office of our pastor. "He's in there. Would you like to talk to him?"

I responded without hesitation. "Please."

The pastor motioned toward a black leather chair. I'd have to face him as I told him that I'd just thrown my ring at my husband and come out as gay. I cried as I explained the details of our fight. Our pastor was a man who knew marriage troubles of his own. He and his wife were always honest, never hiding their own struggles from the church. Maybe that's why the church felt like the safest place for me to drive to that day.

He leaned forward in his chair and clasped his hands together, getting ready to speak to me. I braced myself for what would come next, anticipating his disappointment. *Whatever he's about to say to me*, I thought, *will probably be right*. I would deal with the impact of his words.

I am so broken. Jonathan deserves someone else.

"Lindsey, I'm glad you drove here. I am afraid I don't have the answers you're looking for. But I do know one thing: you need community." I sank. *But I have friends. They cannot solve this.* Was this really all he could give me?

"Let me talk to a few people within our church and see if we can get you a name for someone to talk to." He stood up, and I took that as my cue to go.

"Do you mean, like, a therapist?"

He smiled. "Yes, I think you might benefit from talking to someone." I followed him to the door of his office, and he gestured for me step out first.

But I've been to therapy before, and I felt worse after leaving than I did when I started, I thought.

"I'll be in touch with you, okay?"

I left the church with a prescription to find friends. This was not the advice I was expecting to hear. I was expecting the pastor to have a solution, or to at least give me something tangible to take home to Jonathan. I needed to give Jonathan hope that I'd found a possible cure. I didn't want to go home with nothing.

I was empty-handed and felt no better off walking back into that apartment we shared. I wasn't used to not knowing what we needed to do next. I was a problem solver by nature, answering questions in a black-and-white way; it was either this or that—no in between. I needed my husband to know I was capable of finding the answer.

But what if there is no answer? I began to spiral. *Oh God, I cannot be stuck in this forever.*

We hadn't wanted to tell our friends what was really going on between us, mostly because it's harder to share something you're struggling with when you're in the middle of it. All success stories have difficult moments that have led to the win at the end—but no one talks about the struggle while they're still losing. In my eyes, I was failing, unsure of how much longer I could continue holding on. I did not know when the end would come.

I let myself back inside our apartment and found Jonathan lying on the couch watching TV with our dog. The way he was stretched out made me ache to find my place there, cuddled up right next to him—but I couldn't find the courage to initiate the intimacy. "I'm so sorry," I said as I stepped farther inside our home.

He looked over at me. "I am sorry too." I was surprised to hear him apologize.

You didn't do anything wrong. All of this is my fault.

I took off my wet coat and hung it up in the closet. My dog greeted me, sniffing my feet and then kissing my hands. Jonathan motioned for me to come over to him. I wasn't sure what he was going to ask of me, but I figured he was going to ask me for something. I told myself to just say yes. *Whatever he wants.* I had hurt him enough; the only way he'd really forgive me was to give him whatever he asked for.

He reached for my hand. He could pull me on top of him and I wouldn't budge. *I'll make it through this.* I told my mind to quit thinking. My heart was already numb; only my mind needed to prepare for the moment he would start undressing me. Instead, he held my hand and used my strength to help him sit up. He was sitting before me as I stood in front of him. Then he tilted his chin up to face me.

"Lindsey, will you give me a hug?"

That's all? Just a hug?

I sat on his knee and wrapped my arms around his neck as he hugged my chest. For just this moment, I didn't panic when his body pressed up against mine. I took two deep breaths, the first one soaking in the moment, followed by the one that signaled it was time for him to let go. He read the signals.

"You want to watch *Lost* with me?" His ability to reconcile so quickly, to let it all go without holding onto resentment, well—it was the tie that may have just kept us together. I didn't understand it. How could he not ask me for sex or *anything* at this point? After all I'd just done to hurt him? *Is it true that he just wants to be next to me?* I struggled to believe his motives weren't any more complicated than that.

"Sure." I untied my shoes and sat down, and he invited our dog up on the couch to watch with us. There was nothing to solve today. Nothing we *could* solve today. He seemed to know this already, maybe even before I left the house vowing to come home with an answer. For tonight, all we needed was to remember where we left off on the TV show we watched obsessively together. And in that moment, it was all the redemption I needed.

There was something particularly unique about coming out with the truth. The confession made me feel like I was quitting a drug cold turkey. Maybe it was because I could no longer live in a fantasy. Now that I'd let my husband in, it would be exponentially harder to hide from him again. My story was now a part of his own story. It would be something we faced together, as a married couple. I had never endured this with anyone before; I preferred the hiding.

For days after coming out, I was sick on the couch with what felt like the flu. *I'll never be with a woman again.* This startling reality made me sick to the bone, regretting that I had left Jade the way I did. *I should have been honest with her. I should have told her how much I wanted to be with her.* I wanted her now more than ever.

Every day looked the same. I'd only make it from the bed to the couch before curling my knees up into my chest. The absence felt like agony. Jonathan would go to work and come home to find me in the same position. Sometimes my dog would lie at my feet or on top of the pillows on the couch. I knew he sensed something was off. He was always very attentive to me. Jonathan would come home and sit quietly beside me, like I was sick and he didn't want to make any noise. He offered to rub my back, but I said I'd rather not be touched. He wanted to be close, but he did not know how. I didn't know how either.

Waking up each morning was the hardest part. After Jonathan left the house, I'd fight the urge to leave as well, to go find the closest thing to love to sooth the ache, and to never come home. *I thought our marriage would fix this!* I was so angry that it hadn't. I was helpless in this pain; it was all so much bigger than me. I faced my own powerlessness and wondered if this was what recovery felt like: denying yourself the thing you thought you needed for the life you knew you wanted.

No one held me against my will to stay married. At any moment I could have packed up my things and left. Yet in all the aches and groans, all the temptations to find Jade and beg her to try again, there was always a greater pull within me to stay.

We knew it was time to tell our friends the truth about us. And what our pastor said was also true: we did need a community. They carried us through our first year of marriage. They'd suggest spontaneous outings to get us out of the house and plan weekly *Lost* parties, where we'd sit around the TV and live vicariously through fictional survivors of a plane crash, all alone on an island, trying to figure out how to get back home. It was strangely comforting to watch someone else struggling through anxiety and experiencing the same lack of direction I felt.

I took my pastor's advice and spilled the truth to some close friends—one being a new friend: the woman who had first greeted me inside the church building. She checked on me often, asking me to grab dinner with her or come over for a bonfire night. She and I were the same age, had similar stories, and connected easily. One evening, she and her roommate were going on a walk, and they asked me to come along. We walked and talked as we watched the sun set over our city. They both knew the struggles my marriage faced. They asked me poignant questions on our walk and challenged me to hold on a little longer, hopeful that time would ease some of the burden. And I believed them.

I could give them honest answers, and they'd let me ramble as I processed out loud. They carried my pain with understanding, openhandedly, and with no agenda to persuade me one way or another. On days I wanted to leave him, they'd say, "It's your decision to make, Lindsey . . . and we know how hard this is for you." I would talk through the logistics of divorcing him, but divorce was never as easy as the world made it look.

"If I could take the pain from you, I would," my friend Leslie said to me one morning. We had met for coffee, and I saw the tears in her eyes as we sipped from our respective cups. Of course, I knew she couldn't trade places with me, but I felt loved knowing that she'd willingly ease the burden if she could.

fifteen

Losing Everything

Jonathan and I arrived at an upscale hotel in the middle of Times Square, where we'd spend the next five days together, just him and me. We'd gotten married in December and had wanted a Christmas honeymoon in NYC. And now here we were.

I admired the extravagantly lit Christmas tree next to the concierge's desk as Jonathan greeted the woman behind the counter. While she typed in our names to pull up our reservation, I eagerly shared that it was our honeymoon. She congratulated us as my husband pulled out his credit card to pay for our stay. She typed in the numbers and looked up at us awkwardly. She handed it back. "Your card was declined."

Jonathan took the card back and handed her another one, knowing it was maxed out, too, but hoping by some divine effort from above it'd go through. We could sort out the bigger problem later. She ran the card and gave it back to us, waiting for approval. "I'm sorry. This one was declined too."

I pulled out my phone. "Um, I guess I'll call my dad." I walked to the side of the desk so she could help another guest.

"Dad? Hey, so, for some reason our card was declined and we can't get into our hotel room."

For some reason? Really?

Of course, he knew this was not some rare event or a case of fraudulent activity. We had just arrived at our honeymoon destination, and we didn't have a dime left in our account.

"Okay, hand the phone to the receptionist." He agreed to save us. I handed the phone to the woman behind the desk and let her speak to my father. Jonathan and I waited in embarrassment, fully aware that we were the young kids who really didn't know how to be adults. Already this was proving to be an unfortunate start.

The woman handed me my phone and our set of keys and smiled. "You two enjoy your stay." I thanked my dad and promised to pay him back. Then we walked to the elevator that would lead us to our room for the weekend.

We shuffled our bags into our suite and took a deep breath. The idea was settling in: we were married. We'd been anticipating this moment for six long months. We'd finally arrived, and it all felt a bit foreign. I couldn't figure out what was so different about it, except for the fact that I'd just vowed my life to him, for better or worse. *Vowed my life.* A heavy statement. An enormous commitment. *That* was the difference.

As we unpacked our things, I couldn't help but notice the

king-sized bed and dread the idea of sex. I quickly searched for a way to divert his attention from the same thing I was thinking, though it was naïve of me to believe he hadn't already been thinking about it. It was our honeymoon—the time a couple's expected to have sex more than anything else they do. I rushed to get my coat and asked if he was ready to roam the streets of Times Square. He let my question pass with a shrug, but I was already one foot out the door.

New York at Christmastime was anything but mundane. We eagerly threw ourselves into the magic and the hustle and bustle.

Only a few months prior to saying "I do," we had contemplated calling the whole thing off after a trusted mentor of ours suggested we weren't ready to be married. Both of us desperately wanted our relationship to work, but at what cost? We didn't know. We rushed into the busyness of Manhattan because the volume quieted our doubts. Yet, even in the midst of the noise, the tension of my emotional avoidance was loud and clear.

We stopped inside a local day spa off of Fifth Avenue. Our friends had bought us a couple's massage as a wedding gift, which was a welcome reprieve from conversation. It wasn't until after we left the day spa that I realized I'd forgotten my wedding rings there. I was already falling apart under the pressure to keep up with this new life of commitment. I wasn't used to wearing rings, let alone having one stand for something so significant.

We turned around, but I walked a few steps ahead of Jonathan, frustrated that I was already unfit for this. On the way,

I became embarrassed that I'd have to walk back inside this day spa and be the young girl who didn't care enough about her wedding rings to remember to put them back on after her massage.

I walked into the parlor and there they were, sitting in a little glass bowl at the counter.

"We figured you'd be back," they said.

"Yep," I said bluntly. "Not very used to wearing these things."

I met my husband back outside. "Did you get them?"

Of course I got them, I thought. *I would have said so if I didn't.* My frustration was growing, so I didn't answer him. *Can't he see that I'm scared? That I'm questioning this whole thing? He'll never be able to give me what I need.* There was nothing he could do to steer clear of my current disposition. A simple question from him could set me off in flames of rage.

"Do you want to go to the Christmas market down the street? I found one I think would be nice."

I finally broke. "I don't know where I want to go next! I don't know what I want to do! I don't know that I even want this!"

Forty-eight hours into our marriage, we were yelling at each other in the middle of New York City. No one heard us, or so it seemed. People buzzed by, as if two people screaming at each other was a common occurrence in the city. I threw up my arms as if to cue that I was done, then started walking the opposite direction of my husband. This was starting to look all too familiar. The wedding excitement was over, and I couldn't even enjoy our honeymoon.

But we were no strangers to these types of fights.

We were engaged for six months, and nearly every month

leading up to our wedding day was filled with tough questions, long hours of arguing into the night, struggling through disagreements and unmet expectations, and wondering if we were making the right decision. I was so afraid of a life without him, but I couldn't figure out how to live a life with him either. I thought marriage was the answer, as if it would resolve every issue like magic. I thought everything would start over the day we said "I do." I thought our love would feel like it had before, in those first few months of our knowing each other.

I walked back to our hotel with my husband ten steps behind me. We lay side by side on the bed, frozen in disbelief, wondering what on earth we'd just done.

We spent the next four days pretending. We figured out how to experience the trip together, but at arm's length. No one could have prepared me for the feeling of being trapped. People had tried to warn us that maybe marriage wasn't the best idea for us, but we didn't listen.

I looked into the eyes of this man I'd just married, and it didn't feel like a gain. It felt like I'd just lost everything all at once.

I'd lost the security of doing things my way, being responsible for my own needs and desires. Now there was someone else to consider. The lifeblood of our marriage relied on connecting intimately, and I felt so sickened by the idea that I wanted to cut off the blood source. I felt bound to marriage, like there was no way out. My vulnerability was an unraveling of garments, and I felt naked, and so very afraid, standing before him.

sixteen

Beautiful Addict

Vast Indiana fields gave way to the mercy of a new morning. I rolled my windows down as I drove along the country road to school. I was seventeen years old, wondering if my life had any real purpose anymore. The wind danced through my hair, on a mission to wake up a tired girl.

Orange and yellow hues rose with the sun, turning the sky into a canvas of color. Light burst up from the cold ground below and surrounded me—a stark contrast to the evening before, the one that left my heart so broken I had no tears left to cry. The moment I thought would never come *had* come: the morning I'd wake up and face the day alone. I'd lost Sam, and I feared I'd lose myself now that he was gone. But he wasn't safe anymore.

The sun beamed with her beauty, and I sheltered my eyes from the piercing light. I would need much of her warmth today.

For three years, I'd given Sam all of me. His blue eyes pierced straight through me. I was eager to invite him in, to uncover the most sacred parts of me. I tied my soul to his. He knew all my insecurities and how I'd felt unseen and unloved in the years before we met. His compassion made him so generous in his love for me. Everyone had their own reason for loving Sam, but I was the lucky one who got to share her soul with him.

He was always ready to fight on my behalf. Whenever I had a hard day, stuck in the chronic depression I couldn't yet put a name to, he'd sense something was wrong. He'd rise up in defense and ask, "Did someone say something to you?" I knew he'd confront them, so I'd assure him that no one had; it was just that past wounds still stung.

I fell deeply in love with him—as if love never existed outside of him. He was protective of me, and I felt safest when his arms were wrapped around me. Every anxiety left when I laid next to him, my head on his chest as he played with my hair. He was affectionate and tender. He promised he'd never hurt me. I believed him.

We were young, yes, but never before him had I encountered such a big love between two people. The way he wrote love notes and strategically placed them around school for me to find had me swept up in a frenzy of infatuation.

One evening while we were finishing up dinner together, he pulled a box from his pocket. I already knew what was in it. I opened it to find the most beautiful, simple gold ring. A promise ring. *I promise to love you forever,* he'd tell me. We weren't ready to be married yet, but when we were old enough, we'd do it right away.

But soon, I watched as his promise began to fade.

I remembered back to our first date—when I was fourteen and he was sixteen—and the moment he pulled a small bit of LSD from his pocket. He saw how upset I was about it and promised he was only holding onto it for a friend. I'd never seen drugs before—never even associated with people who smoked cigarettes.

The signs had been there all along—but so was his love.

Three years later, the truth came in sobering clarity. I couldn't escape the truth: Sam was an addict. The boy I had fallen in love with was gone.

I frantically searched his eyes for something to hold onto. Was there any promise left in him? His eyes shifted from left to right, and he couldn't keep steady on his feet. I wanted to shake him out of it. *Where are you?* I silently pleaded. Maybe I could pull him out, one last time. When I'd seen the first signs—the copious amounts of weed he was selling, the prescription pills he'd hidden, and the call I'd received just after midnight from the county jail—I'd hoped my love would change him. But Sam was caught somewhere deep inside of himself. Somewhere no one was allowed to enter. Somewhere painful, I presumed.

I listened to him slur his words. He moved in to kiss me, but I pulled away. He noticed. I watched him disappear. How could I grieve the loss of someone still standing right in front of me? If I beat on his chest, would it revive him? Would he even feel it? Would anyone listen to me if I called for help? *We're going to lose him!* But I'd alluded to his problem before; no one seemed to listen. Where was the boy who was once wild with romance? The boy who had once been full of poetry now had none left in him.

Maybe out of everything, I grieved the loss of his mind the most. He was so brilliant and charming and well-spoken—but his mind grew dark. He saw demons in his house and called the police in frantic panics. You wouldn't have believed me if I told you he once could light up a room.

In the earlier days, when I'd question him, he'd promise he wasn't high. But he was a master at lying—"to keep me safe," so he said. After all, he said he never wanted to hurt me—though those words were starting to mean nothing to me anymore. His eyes told me everything I never wanted to know. The whites of his eyes were stained red. His pupils expanded wider every minute the drug was in his body. He couldn't hide anymore. And he was no longer safe for me to hide in.

I got him to sit down, finally, so I could try to talk to him one last time. He pulled out a piece of paper and scribbled down a few words. He held it up to the light and slurred his speech as he read the words back to me. I listened, quietly, as the tears spilled down my cheeks. He'd written me one last poem. *He's choosing this*, I reminded myself, knowing I'd asked him months ago to find help and he'd refused. I knew it was time to say goodbye.

When he finished reading his note, he saw my tears. He ran his fingers through my hair and told me he'd always love me. But I did not believe him anymore. His addiction was stronger than his love. He would have stopped using a long time ago if it wasn't.

He walked me to my car and shut the door behind me. I wasted no time before pulling away from the house. What was once a fairytale dream had come to an end—in total despair. *You are not worth the fight*, his choice had spoken to me. *My God, how do I live without him?*

I rolled down the window and breathed the night air in deep. It smelled bright of Indiana cornfields, and it reminded me of the drives we took together. He'd split his focus between me and the road, but my focus was only on him. He'd catch me looking at him, smile, and kiss my hand intertwined with his.

But that was all over now. No more late-night drives or sweet kisses. I leaned back on the headrest behind me and pushed my toes further into the gas pedal. *Forget the memories.* Apathy was my refuge now. I eyed a telephone pole. *Your life is over.* Ten-and-two. My grip loosened. My fingers let go, one by one. *Just do it.* That same deceitful voice now roared like a lion.

You are not loved. You have no purpose.

Faster, I pushed. Sixty miles an hour on a narrow country road. The first telephone pole passed by me with a flash. There was another coming up. Palms sweating. But then I heard a new sound: *You are not far from home, Lindsey.*

Just go home.

I gasped, then let out a loud cry. I let up on the gas and passed the last telephone pole. Loud, groaning sobs broke through the apathy. He was gone. Every part of my future I'd planned included him, but there was no returning to him. Another two miles, and I turned off on the road toward home.

My dad was waiting up for me, as he always did. His concerned eyes watched me walk by him like a ghost. His daughter, so far away. I crawled upstairs and sank into the soft sheets of my full-sized bed. The bed felt too big. What I would have given to have a smaller bed, with no room to toss and turn. What I would have done to have someone in this bed holding me. My tears led to a deep sleep. When I woke up, the pain started all over again, and I could hardly breathe.

A few weeks after Sam and I broke up, I went out for the first time without him. I showed up to a party and could feel the absence of him on my arm. The void was unmissable. The music shook the walls and pulsed through my chest the moment I stepped into the house. Loud voices from the other room resembled that of a drunken fraternity. *Boys*, I thought with disgust. Why I committed to meeting my friends at this party, I didn't know.

I witnessed his friends throw back shot after shot. Vodka, mostly. Vodka made them loud and unsettling. I despised drunk men, or maybe I despised the way I felt around drunk men—unsafe, unprotected—but especially around his friends. The friends who took advantage of his habits for their own selfish gain. They kept his habit going, kept his supply coming. But they were not the only ones, I suppose. Still, resentment tainted my blood. I could do with never seeing another one of his friends again.

I found an empty barstool and passed on the shot offered to me. My friends were taking theirs though. I saw no point in trying to start a conversation as everyone was already yelling over each other. Alcohol made people do that. The more shots one took, the less aware they were of themselves and their sound level. The pain in my heart was all too present anyway, vying for my attention; I didn't want to talk.

My friends stayed close like they said they would, but I was alone in my feelings. They were pardoned from the heartache and were laughing and dancing. I scanned the room, and my eyes found Sam's friend staring at me. He threw back his shot and slapped the glass on the counter. He was a sloppy drunk, slobbering and spitting with every word that came from his mouth. He could hardly keep steady as he stood there. He leaned his arm on the bar and pointed at me.

"You." He slobbered. "You bitch." I heard his words, but it was the hate in his eyes that demanded my attention. "It's your fault he's not here. Your fault he turned out the way he did."

My friend Emily stepped in-between he and I. Although she was inches shorter than him, she was far bigger in my mind. "Leave her alone," she said. I kept still on the stool. It was safer to remain numb, to not let him see my hurt.

He moved in closer and sneered. "You were never good for him."

I was growing angry at his blame. He hadn't witnessed the moments that I showed up to Sam's house to talk him out of a rampage, him shooting his gun out the window at imaginary monsters down below, or the moments I had lain next to him as he called me another girl's name. He didn't know of the times I visited Sam in the psychiatric hospital, bringing him a blanket because he was sober enough to tell me how cold he was at night. Maybe if he knew that, he wouldn't hate me so much. But what did it matter? He wouldn't care even if I tried to explain it. I tried everything I could to save Sam. I had loved him the most. But from this friend's perspective, I was the one guilty. His words had finally broken me and I told my friends I was leaving.

Maybe it is my fault. Maybe I was never good enough for him.

I slid my eyes up from the floor, motioning to Jen that that was the end. "He called me when I was engaged to Jonathan. He asked me for one more chance. He was sober, at least I thought he was based on the sound of his voice . . . But I told him that I was in love with Jonathan and I'd given him every chance in the world. I told him no."

"Did it hurt to talk to him again?" Jen asked.

"No. Jonathan is every good thing Sam was, and more. I had made peace with the loss of Sam, but I think he was just getting sober enough to realize I was already gone."

A small piece of paper slid underneath the french doors and interrupted the moment. Jen smirked as she saw her seven-year-old daughter run back into the other room where her dad was sitting. Her daughter had made something and wanted to show us. Her lighthearted, precious spirit broke my sadness. Jen got out of her seat and reached for the letter. When she opened it, she grinned and handed it over to me. "It's for you," she said. I took the paper from her and opened it up. It was a purple flower. I was so taken by the simplicity in her thoughtfulness it made me cry. I placed the piece of paper safely inside my journal and told Jen to tell her daughter that her drawing for me was like a great big bear hug, and it came at the best time.

Jen paused and asked me how I was feeling.

"The work you're doing is *hard* work, Lindsey." She was right, it wasn't easy to uncover a previous life you'd kept purposefully hidden. Most days, after leaving her house, I'd go home and sleep for hours. From head to heart, I was exhausted—but I'd concluded that the work was worth it.

"Do you want to talk about what happened in our last session?" Jen was sensitive in her delivery. The day before, I'd abruptly ended our session an hour early after crying, "It's all just too hard!" before walking out her front door.

The vulnerability. The ache of remembering. Going home to a marriage that was still so complicated, yet still fighting for every good, celebratory moment to come by. It all overwhelmed me. I apologized for leaving so quickly, but she assured me that hard days are welcome too. "How are you in this moment?" She asked. "I am okay, actually. I am feeling . . . peace."

Letting Jen see me in those more honest, vulnerable moments was something I was still getting comfortable with. Vulnerability had been a foreign concept before I stepped into her home. I'd kept a hard exterior, never wanting to appear weak—and my understanding of a softness, of crying, was that it was weak to show that side of ourselves. But Jen was showing me something different. She was showing me that I could be loved amid my tears, that being vulnerable was the furthest thing from being weak. She was showing me that honesty is a light, and I wouldn't be left alone in the dark so long as one of us had a light.

seventeen

Rain

I searched frantically for my keys. I'd forgotten where I put them. I was turning pockets inside out and checking every surface in our home for where I may have set them. Jonathan looked concerned.

"You shouldn't drive this upset." I ignored him and didn't slow my pace.

"I'm a horrible wife." There. I'd said it out loud.

"You're not a horrible wife, Lindsey." He was always trying to encourage me. Maybe he was more afraid of what would happen if he wasn't there to dismantle that lie.

I found the keys inside the pocket of the sweatshirt I'd worn the night before. *I've got to get out of here.* I passed Jonathan on my way out. He wasn't going to stop me, and I knew this because he had never tried stopping me before. I shut the door behind me and raced to the car. Sometimes I wished he would run after me, maybe wrestle me to the ground. Fighting was an easy reaction for me when I felt anger. But he never fought me. He never once laid a finger on me. But most times, his gentleness was infuriating.

I had no idea of where I'd go. I just knew I needed to drive.

The farther away I got from home, the more I cried. It's not easy to drive when you're crying—at least, not as hard as I was. This was a deep, belly-level cry. The kind that releases the tears from years ago, all stuffed beneath layer after layer of other weighty things.

Jen and I had been digging. All the pain I had buried was being uncovered. I was grieving things lost, maybe for the first time ever. I was like a child all over again, taking my pain out on the one who loved me most.

Weeks before, observing the tiredness we both faced in a marriage loaded with strife, I had asked Jonathan, "Why won't you just leave me?" Those words preceded the moment we'd found our way back to each other, after the anger finally left and I acknowledged I was just terribly afraid he actually *would* leave. I crawled into his arms, and we sat together and cried.

"Because I don't want to leave you," he had said. He hugged me tighter. "You keep thinking I'm going to leave you, but I am still sitting right here."

He wasn't the flight risk. It was always me—the one afraid of facing the inevitable pain of digging through a lifetime of heartache purposefully kept hidden. But what I was learning was that wherever I went, the pain would follow me until I forced myself to look it square in the face.

While driving, I wiped the tears from my eyes. Up on my

left, there was a church parking lot that looked empty. I turned in there and drove to the side of the lot that faced an empty field. I put my car in park and cracked my windows. I laid my seat back just enough to rest my head. It was finally safe to cry, but I was all out of tears.

I stared toward the field and noticed the sky turning gray. A storm began to roll in. It hadn't reached me yet, but it would soon—though I wasn't anxious to get home. Storms didn't scare me anyway. I closed my eyes and took in a few deep breaths. I offered myself reassuring thoughts: *It won't always be so hard.* It didn't feel easy now, but I promised myself it would get easier.

The rain hit my windshield as the smell of a summer storm ushered its way in. To me, nothing is more soothing than the smell of rain. I turned my car on just long enough to roll up my windows. Then I noticed a newly built pavilion on the church property. It had a slab of concrete and a roof, and I wanted to ride out the storm beneath it.

The rain picked up, and I heard a far-off cry of thunder. I took my shoes off and left my socks hidden inside them, then looked around me to make sure I was still alone. I put my keys on the dashboard and stepped out of the car.

My toes felt the rough pavement underneath them before I made my way toward the tall, wet grass. I embraced the oneness of a world where everything had a purpose as my naked feet met the naked earth. I walked through the grass, taking my time as the water ran over my head and soaked my T-shirt. The feeling of anything other than my own emotional pain was well received.

My life had hit a point where I could no longer control it, though maybe it was the illusion of control that I had actually lost. Do we ever really have control over our lives the way we think we do? Just as the rain covered me from head to toe—with no authority of my own to direct the flow of the water—so it was with my healing. I was simply a body, held captive by a love that would uncover me, pour over me, and leave me different than I was before. I could only embrace it or run from it.

I embraced the storm like I embraced love. Reckless, and not without risk.

I reached the pavilion and hesitated to step under its cover. To stand out from under it felt a little wild and freeing. My footprints from the wet, muddy land covered the slab of concrete as if I were claiming this new territory. I heard the echo of thunder and rain circling the A-frame roof above me, and I met the sound in harmony with my own voice.

What can wash away my sin?

Nothing but the blood of Jesus.

I repeated it louder, finding relief in the expression.

I walked to the edge of the shelter and looked to the distance. *God, please, will you show yourself to me?* I wanted to see him, to see Jesus walk over to me, walking toward me from the farthest part of the trees. He could take me back with him; I didn't care. I was desperate to see him, to have him make everything make sense.

Am I not here with you already? His voice echoed in my ears, in unison with the song, the rain, and the tears.

I looked above me and noticed a little sparrow flying from

beam to beam. He was seeking shelter from the storm too. Or maybe he had heard me singing and the melody of a song he already knew drew him there. I looked back out at the field and saw no one coming. I took a deep breath and knew that this waiting was not all for nothing—that all the pain and all the searching would one day turn into a story worth telling. So, I stepped out from the pavilion again, finding freedom in relinquishing myself to the rain—a force I could not control.

It was time to go back home.

I pulled into the driveway and let myself inside our house. Jonathan was sitting on the couch reading. He said hi to me and was visibly relieved I had come home. He noticed I was all wet, but it may have been the smile on my face that stood out more. I sat down next to him before I went to change my clothes. "I'm sorry I left like I did. I just needed to get out, needed to drive." He listened attentively as I shared my experience.

"I'm glad you took the space you needed for yourself. But I've been really struggling . . ."

I had left the house to work through my restlessness, and because I'd worked through it in *my* mind, I thought I could go back home to everything being normal again. Civil.

"I'm afraid I'm going to lose you," he said as his voice cracked. "I don't know how to help you when you spiral like that." He was now being vulnerable, sharing a tender part of himself.

I held his hand and gave him my best attempt at assurance that I would be okay in the end. "I know it scares you." I didn't know how he could help me either. I was learning how to feel again and leaning into the grief I never allowed myself to experience before. "It scares me too."

That was the truth. I was afraid of losing myself too. But scarier than standing face-to-face with the pain of my past was a future void of love and belonging. I figured, just as I'd seen amid that day's rain, I had more beauty than pain to discover. It was out there, somewhere.

eighteen

Two Lines

It was a month into the New Year, and Jonathan and I had just made it to our one-year anniversary. The burden of our inactive sex life was heavy on my shoulders; we were not that different from casual roommates—though now I wonder if some casual roommates still slept together more often than we did. However, a month before on New Year's Eve—due to either the vodka, the endorphins, or just a general desire to have sex—Jonathan and I managed to put aside our disconnectedness and come together as married couples do.

I don't remember much of that night after the sex. I only remember the evening leading up to it. I remember hosting our friends from Hawaii that evening, playing cards with them for hours, and pouring hefty doses of Grey Goose into our cranberry juice. We laughed a lot, as we always did with them. Even though Jonathan and I struggled to find our way together, we still knew how to have a good time as friends.

But as I try to remember that night, my guess is that—in the moment—I was far too elated to focus on all the ways I was failing him as a wife. He and I were just cutting loose, laughing, and having fun.

The burden of sex wasn't as heavy after a good night of fun. As such, I didn't struggle to let my husband intimately close to me that night. It was never the sex itself that scared me, but the undressing—the part where he'd uncover all the delicate parts of me.

A few weeks later, I caught myself in the mirror. *I am not panicked. I am hopeful. Could this really be happening?* I placed the test on the counter and shut the bathroom door behind me. *I can't stay in here and watch it.* I went to my bedroom and plopped down on the bed. I had two minutes to wait until I'd discover what was happening inside my body, but I'd sensed it for a week now. I was pregnant.

I have always known I'd be a mother. It was never something I'd been confused about. As a matter of fact, parenting was the only thing I was confident I'd be good at. Nurture. Tenderness. Holding a sleeping infant on my chest while I laid as still as possible, feeling the deep breaths of their tiny chest rise and fall on mine. Someone to call my own. Someone to call me *Mom. What will she look like?* I was already seeing her face in my mind. *Or will it be a boy? A little version of Jonathan?* The anticipation of having and holding our tiny child made me wonder if parenthood might create a stronger attachment between Jonathan and me.

I took a deep breath and walked back into the bathroom.

It had barely been two minutes, but surely the test would be ready. What I had sensed was confirmed when I saw two lines on the plastic test stick.

We're having a baby.

I paced the tiny bathroom and began thinking of every possible way to break the news to Jonathan. I wondered how he'd take it. He was always so worried about us, trying everything he could to keep the focus on strengthening our bond. Would a child mess that up?

As for me, all the worries of whether my marriage would survive vanished at the thought of having our first child together. I took the pregnancy test, carefully wrapped it in tissue, and set it on the back of the toilet. Perhaps keeping it for proof would help Jonathan believe me. Otherwise, he might think I was playing a joke on him. *Why do men think this anyway? As if a woman would joke about carrying a human life inside of her.*

We had been watching a movie together when I slipped out, and now Jonathan was calling for me, asking where I'd gone. I hollered down at him from upstairs. "Be down in a second!"

I locked our bedroom door and tore a piece of paper from my journal. I struggled with how to tell him. He would likely cry, and the movie we'd been watching wouldn't matter anymore. *Do I wait to tell him? I cannot wait to tell him.* Would he feel scared to be a parent? I decided to preemptively address those fears in my letter: "You'll be a great father. We'll figure out the money later. You and I will keep trying in our marriage; I'm not giving up yet."

I searched my thoughts for some really good way to end the letter, but all I could think to write was, "I can't believe we're going to be parents. I love you so much."

I dug through my sock drawer for the tiny bib I'd bought just days ago, when I first had a feeling. I had been keeping it secret, still wrapped in the shopping bag I brought it home in. Since I didn't have a gift bag, I just hid it behind my back.

As I walked down the stairs with one arm tucked behind me, he saw the note in my other hand.

"What's that?"

I grinned at him and sat down. "I just want you to read it."

I handed him the letter, then observed his body language. He sat perfectly still as he read the letter and then read it again. He looked up at me as I sat there nervously, smiling in his direction. He lowered the letter into his lap, and I noticed the tears welling in his eyes.

"You're pregnant?"

"I am." I took my hand out from behind my back and gave him the bib. He laughed when I handed it to him. I could tell he was nervous, likely thinking of all the logistics now that he'd have another individual to care for.

Not only that, but Jonathan could never be certain I'd stay in our relationship—and I could give him no real assurance other than the reality that I'd stayed today and hoped to stay again tomorrow. Another day with each other was never guaranteed. Now a child would be part of our relational uncertainty, but I'd never felt more hopeful. Maybe a new baby would only be one part of this gift. Something of deeper significance was growing between us, while *she* grew inside of me.

He pulled me into the crook of his arm, and I let him hold me. *We're gonna be okay*, I thought.

nineteen

Wrestling God

The clock read one o'clock, and I was restless in bed. I'd become familiar with the racing thoughts that flooded my mind once the night grew silent. The busyness of the day protected me from the swarm of questions nagging me for answers.

We'd made it through three years of marriage and had our first baby girl. Life together, now as a family of three, was still moving forward, but I felt only half alive. My heart was still torn in two, desiring the man I chose forever with and the woman I so desperately wanted to be near.

This will be a long night, I thought. I closed my heavy eyes, desperate to let my memory fade. I tossed and turned along with the stirring in my heart. I was missing her—again. *Why is this so hard?* I became too angry to rest. Something in me felt destructive. *Why is this not fixed!* I could not rest with a mind that was spiraling. I sat up and tugged the chain on the light, then reached for a pen and took my angst out in the journal Jen had given me long ago. The pages were almost full now, but here I was, still stuck with the same questions and burdens I could not release. The thought of still being *here* made me want to cry. *It just hurts so bad*, I'd write—but I was praying now. *Oh God, will this feeling ever go away?* In the end, whether it did or whether it didn't, I was most desperate for just one miracle: *God, please let me love my husband.*

I got up and paced the space on my side of the bed. I weighed divorce against our current state. Would it be better to just end the marriage? Giving in felt easier than the oppressive guilt I experienced as a wife who could not give herself fully to her husband. But then I thought of our beautiful, brown-eyed daughter, who effortlessly loved her mommy and daddy with all she had in her. It broke me to think about a separated life for her, where all the new memories she made would now be torn in two. I could accept the breaking of our marriage, but not the breaking of our child. *But don't you want out of this?*

Of course I wanted out of the loneliness. But if I wasn't going to leave him, what was the way forward? *I could lie to him*, I thought. *He'd never know.* My thoughts began to justify my desires. Yet even then, I felt paralyzed by the idea of carrying a lie for so long. I looked over at the man asleep in bed—the one who, after all the unknowns, had still chosen to lay beside me. If I was feeling lonely, then what must he be feeling? The panic in my heart began to settle at the thought of him feeling the desperation too. Two people, stuck in the same loneliness, having nothing to give each other. I pressed my hand to my chest and rubbed the ache in my heart.

I knelt down, one knee at a time, folding my body over my legs, palms turned up. Surrendered. *Here I am, Jesus. Have your way.* Dawn began to break.

The next morning, we dropped off our daughter in the church nursery. Jonathan and I were holding the community around us at arm's length; we'd had a rough morning. We walked into church and sat in a corner away from any overhead lights. It felt good to be hidden from the crowd. I listened to the pastor talk about how we can live a life of freedom through our relationship with God. He spoke about it so freely, like that freedom was available for everyone. But to me, his words fell flat. I felt the anger stirring inside me. *I've done everything I was supposed to do, and I do not feel very free.* I was still stuck with no way forward but to get out of bed, every single day, and do the best I could.

I looked around at the church full of people—people who mostly knew my and my husband's story. I pushed back the resentment that grew every time someone sitting near me nodded in agreement with the pastor's words. *Look at them, with their healthy new marriages and thriving family lives.* I grew cold. I nudged my husband in the side and asked if we could leave.

We found a spot on the ground outside the church where we could sit until it was time to pick up our daughter. The stillness agitated me. Now I had nothing to distract my thoughts—not that being inside the church was any better. It wasn't. I was still caught up in the arguments between Jonathan and me from the days before. The same dissension between us that told me: *This marriage will never work out.*

The silence lingered. *Why is it that I keep hearing about this "freedom" God offers, but I am still trapped inside myself?* My husband let me work out my thoughts in the quiet. I'd become defensive toward God. *You don't offer me freedom, God. You just leave me in the pain.* I'd finally confronted him. The anger, the resentment, had come to the surface.

You never loved me.

I believed that at some point when I was a child, God looked at me and decided I wasn't worth the fight. He had abandoned me. *I'll never measure up*, I thought.

The pavement was rough on my legs as I crossed them in front of me. I raised my hands up to cover my face, feeling the tears about to fall. My husband put his hand on my back to comfort me. I was desperate for answers and had none. I was newly married, a new mother to a little girl who needed the very love and affection that I felt completely deficient in. I could not give her what I did not have to give.

I needed a promise from God: an insight into his world and what he was up to in mine. I needed a dramatic change of course in my life. I needed him to come down from the heavens and tell me face-to-face that he hadn't left me. I fought hard to discover the truth outside those church walls.

As Jonathan sat patiently next to me, I shared my thoughts out loud.

"Do you think God would *really* abandon me? Because it just feels like he has. I mean, is he that sick of me?"

My husband's voice broke through his own stillness.

"I don't think he's ever abandoned you."

He pulled out his small pocket journal—the one he took notes in from time to time when he read something he liked in a book, or the sermon was good on a Sunday morning. He read, "From an aerial view, it's hard to tell whether two people are wrestling or making love. The idea is that they are so close, it's hard to tell the difference."

I let the words sink in. It was hard for me to understand love as an act of wrestling because love as I had understood it was supposed to be easy, feel-good, and passionate. It was supposed to be *natural.* What had never occurred to me before was that, perhaps, love comes through the wrestle. Maybe God hadn't abandoned me; maybe his love was right there in the struggle.

What once seemed like a hopeless future had started to shift now in my mind. I let Jonathan in on my thoughts. "What if there is purpose in all of this? All the ache, the disappointment, the emptiness and loneliness . . . the pain?" I looked up and saw tears form in his eyes. How long had they been there? I didn't know. "What if the wrestle is exactly what's moving us into love?" I leaned into my husband. He was quiet in his own battle that day, choosing to hold me in his arms until church let out.

twenty

Flying Free

I took my time on the drive over to Jen's home. I was awakening to the world around me, becoming alive with clarity. Not a clarity that comes with specific answers, but a clarity of love. One that says, "Whether today holds joy or pain, you are loved." It was the middle of winter, and the sky was a light gray. There was a chance of snow, but I didn't count on it. Snow predictions in Tennessee could only be hoped for, never planned on.

I turned the music up and let it play loudly over my car speakers. The music centered me, like it was pulling on the corset strings of my heart. I was held together in the melody.

When I arrived, I gave Jen a tight hug and sat down on the love seat. "You're glowing," she said. Was I? I let out a laugh, not sure how to respond to such a statement. Yet somehow, I believed her.

I felt free—or a little freer than in days past. I wasn't sure what was causing me to feel so happy, but it had almost happened overnight. I just woke up, and the magic had finally arrived. I didn't stop to consider that maybe it was a result of the hours we'd spent together for the last five months, creating free space in my heart for love. I was so busy digging and digging, as if the digging would never end—but maybe my shovel had hit a surface. What was left for me to uncover? I was finding a freedom that came with exposing the dirt in my life, but nothing compares to the freedom of having nothing left to hide.

She smirked at me and set her notebook and pencil down. "I've noticed a change in you. You are not the same woman who walked in this room five months ago." I took an internal inventory. *Yes. I feel totally different.* "And I think you are ready."

Ready for what?

"I don't think you need me like you used to."

"Really?" I said, surprised.

"How do you feel about that?" she asked.

Afraid, I thought, *but maybe a little bit intrigued.* "I don't like losing people I care about."

"You're not losing me, Linds." She was attuned to my fear of loss.

But the truth was, I hadn't solved every issue in my marriage. We had uncovered so much, yet I felt like there was still a lifetime of work ahead of me. *How can she be so sure?* Loose ends needed to be tied up: like my debilitating fear. There were questions I didn't have the answers to, even still. And the lingering doubt that I would buckle under the pressure of it all still remained. Yet amid all my questioning, I felt a stirring within my heart that I could trust the process of healing.

Maybe there isn't a reality in which all the loose ends are tied up as we move forward. There is no such thing as a figured-out life. Life is always moving, morphing, offering us something to learn in the joy and sadness of our everyday moments. Instead, maybe Jen knew it was time for her to pull back, because I was now heading toward the place we'd set our sights on in the very beginning: the place where I was most myself. Most free. Most unashamed. Most loved.

I looked up at her and smiled. "Actually, I think you might be right."

We were ending an era, or so it felt. Though I had only known Jen for five months, it felt like we'd been acquainted since the beginning of time. Few people in our lives will so willingly enter the dark night of our souls the way she entered mine.

I sat up from the love seat and pulled at the loose ends of my sweater. *I guess this is really the end.* She stood to her feet and stretched out her arms for a hug, and I hugged her tight. "Thank you," I said. Those two words fell short of the gratitude I really felt. In the beginning, she had told me I could trust her with my broken heart, and she'd proven it was true.

I noticed a light snow falling outside the windows. She must have seen me spot it because she turned around to look for herself. "Fitting, isn't it?" she said with a grin—the beauty of a first snowfall symbolizing a change in season for me. Together, we watched the white flakes fall in slow motion, and I anticipated the moment I would open Jen's front door, step outside, and feel the tiny snowflakes grazing my skin. *Fitting, it is.*

"You have my number," she said as I gathered up my things.

"I do. And I'll talk to you soon," I said, trying to hint that I did not want to lose touch, before I walked out her front door for the last time. Goodbyes were never easy for me. I had a feeling we were both going to miss the time we spent together. I sighed and we smiled, hugging each other one last time. She and I both knew moments would soon come when I would be desperate for answers, but I'd have to trust in my own inner guide.

She opened the front door, and we both delighted in the cold air hitting our skin. She wrapped her sweater around her body and crossed her arms to keep warm. I raised the hood of my jacket over my head and stepped out. It was just me now. Me and the world in front of me. Fresh snow. New territory. I turned my palms up to catch the snow in my hands. I lifted my face toward the sky and closed my eyes, receiving those purifying flakes as they landed gently on my skin. One by one, they kissed my eyelids, welcoming me as a new woman, with a new identity, into the same ol' world I started in.

A winter of cold temps and rainy days left everyone eager for spring. I enjoyed sipping my coffee in the mornings from the treehouse Jonathan and his dad had built. There was a bird's nest safely positioned underneath it, in a nook of two support beams. A very smart bird to choose such a sturdy location. I'd carefully watched the bird nest from its start. Mama Robin had crafted a beautiful, safe place to lay her eggs, nurturing her young well before they hatched. Once they began to break free from their shells, I remember how scared I was that another animal would hurt them. I observed this Mama Robin for a month, seeing her sneak out early in the morning for food while I sipped my coffee, trying hard not to disturb her.

She did what she needed to do, flying back with each new seed, worm, or berry, and feeding it to her young. When another bird or squirrel stalked nearby, she would fly aggressively at them, giving them no time to defend an attack. Once she even darted at my kids. I forgave her and told my kids to keep their distance, explaining to them that she was doing exactly what she was created to do: protect and nurture her nest, and give her babies a safe place to grow.

I found a way to spy on the babies that safeguarded me from the beak of their mother. I quietly climbed the treehouse steps and walked over until I stood right above them. I snuck my phone in between the slats of the decking, sliding my phone down just enough to catch a direct view of the nest with my camera.

Daily, I checked on my baby birds and watched them grow. I have videos from when their eyes were barely open to the moment they started to fill in with feathers—awkward coats they struggled to fit into before their bodies grew big enough.

But one day I went out there and the birds were gone. I panicked for a moment until I realized they must have gotten their wings and flown away. I left the nest alone, hoping to keep their home intact in case they needed to come back. But after a few days, I was raking up pine straw by the treehouse and noticed the nest had fallen. Maybe the wind had blown it down, or maybe it fell without the weight of the birds holding it down. Regardless, there was no life left in that nest.

At times I would grow a little homesick for the mansion in the hills, the nest I was nurtured in. But maybe this is how God had always set it up. When the chaos resurfaced, I could always escape back to those intimate memories, sitting there on the love seat, when the world had grown quiet and love had become loud. Though it had been time for me to leave Jen, I was still afraid of the world in front of me. I wondered if the baby birds had been scared too.

All of this had made me question how often I look for God, or security, in a place God has already moved on from. Not because he has left me, though, but because perhaps he is leading me someplace new. I thought about Jen's home, her guidance, and how I would have stayed there for longer than I was ever supposed to. I might have leaned on her, depended on her, forever. Never finding the excitement a new trail would lead to, with feet that still walk even when they don't know where they're headed.

There is something really mystifying about not knowing the path you're on but trusting the Spirit that leads you. The Spirit never stays in the same place for long. I have found God to be more playful as we've journeyed together, peeking his head around the trees when I get lost, beckoning me to continue following him. I never see him, but I'll yell back, "Okay, I'm coming! But could you slow down a bit?" I may not know where I'm going, but I know who I'm following—and I will keep moving my feet.

twenty-one

Come Close

There were months I prayed to see Jade again. *Just one more time, Jesus. Please.* It was less of a request and more of a desperate plea. Of course, I never thought he'd actually answer that prayer. I imagined he'd reply: *What good would it do to see her again?*

I, of course, had no logical explanation to give God, but that didn't keep me from trying to persuade him anyway. "Because then I'll know!" I had yelled at him, out loud, in the middle of my bedroom, crying with a pen in my hand and a journal in front of me. The confusion was so thick it made my head swim. But what else did I *really* need to know? What could I learn from running into her again that I hadn't known already? That my heart was attached to a love I could no longer receive? I already knew that. But there was no escaping the grief of losing it.

I wanted to stay lost in the fantasy. *She can soothe the pain, even if for just a moment.* I pressed my hand into my chest and gripped my shirt, making a fist over my heart. My attempt to apply pressure to the wound. How natural of a reaction this is: that whenever we feel pain, we instinctively apply pressure—as if the wound itself is begging to be held tightly. *Wrap me up and hold me tight. Don't let me go until I feel better.* I kept a hand pressed to my chest.

It was a cloudy afternoon, and I was on day two of a head cold that had all but knocked me out. Still, my nephew's birthday had just passed, and I needed to mail his gifts to him. I piled the presents in my hands, knowing I'd need to grab a ready-to-mail box at the post office to ship them in. I approached the front door right as a nice, tall man held it open for a woman who also had her hands full—except hers held a baby carrier and mine held a wrapped Nerf gun and extra Nerf bullets. I thanked him as I snuck in right after the woman, giving him a nod before he let the door shut behind me.

I was shuffling through boxes trying to find the right size, noting that large Nerf guns are not as easy to ship as one might think. I was not trying to make a mess of things, but I needed to put some of the boxes together to make sure my items would fit before I walked to the counter. The post office runs a tight ship, and if you're not ready when it's your turn, everyone behind you will hate you for it.

I was sifting through the boxes on the floor when I heard

someone behind me say my name. "Hey, Lindsey." I turned around and noticed her eyes first. Jade. I stood up abruptly and fixed my hair, hoping I didn't look as disheveled as I felt.

"Wow! Hey! What are you doing here?" *That was a dumb thing to say. What are any of us doing here at the post office besides the obvious?*

"I'm picking up a package I had delivered here." *Obviously.* She pulled out a small box and said, "You wanna see something?" She walked over to the counter and found an empty space just behind the customers in line. Then she motioned for me to come over.

Is this really happening?

After all that time, and despite how things ended, she was treating me like everything was normal. I, on the other hand, had been dreaming of this moment. This was supposed to be the moment when everything would make sense: when I would look at her and be swept away. Why was she being so casual? We had finally found each other again. Had she not been thinking of me like I was thinking of her?

She took a key and cut through the tape on the box. Opening it, she reached inside for a smaller black box. She pulled it out, and I immediately noticed its shape. There is only one item that fits into a box that size. "I am proposing to my girlfriend," she said, lifting the lid to release the glow of the diamond.

Oh God. I watched her eyes light up and tried to find the words to congratulate her.

"To Lex?" I asked, confused.

"No, we broke up after you left." My gaze slid down to the

floor. *Yeah, about that. Is this the moment I tell her about that kiss? Do I just say it?*

"So, what do you think? Will she like it?" She was wanting my approval.

Am I seeing what could have been mine? Or am I blowing this completely out of proportion? I was drowning in the waterfall of my own imagination. Nothing I'd envisioned was happening. I smiled at her, but I felt empty.

I noticed the way my heartbeat picked up in my chest.

This is really the end.

I knew in my heart that this was the last time we'd ever see each other.

I locked eyes with her. "I think the ring is really, really beautiful." I wondered if I should take her hand in mine when I said this, adding sentiment to a moment that would be the end. But I didn't. "She is a lucky woman."

She closed the box and looked back at me. "Thanks." She paused. "It was good to see you, Lindsey." I heard the sincerity in her voice. I wondered if she was recognizing the rarity of this moment too. *Good? Yeah, maybe, and hard.* "You have my number . . . so, don't be a stranger." She cracked a smile.

I deleted your number. I had to.

"Yeah, okay . . . I won't," I lied. "Take care of yourself. And, um, congratulations on the engagement." I dug deep to say it. I really wanted to mean it. I wanted to wrap my arms around her like I'd dreamed about doing all these years, to test and see if what I'd felt was even real—but I didn't. Then, she left.

I didn't watch her walk away. Instead, I turned around

and finished picking up the boxes I'd left on the floor, trying to redirect my focus. *Maybe I didn't need this.* I forgot, for a moment, why I prayed for this. *You knew if I saw her, it might crush me again*, I spoke to God. *You knew she was not thinking about me like I was thinking about her. My thoughts were nothing more than fantasy.* The humiliation kicked in. *Why would she want me?* . . .

I picked up my Nerf guns, now secured inside a shipping box that would cost me double the price of the items themselves. I fell in place at the back of the line, sure everyone had just witnessed our exchange. I felt the heat of their attention and tried not to make eye contact. *They can hear my thoughts; I am sure of it.*

All I wanted now was to run home, crawl into bed, and forget everything I'd ever known. *God, I am a fool.* I heard no sound, no encouragement, no opposition, but only the word, "Next!" being yelled out into the room. It was my turn.

"Is there anything hazardous, liquid, metal . . ." The woman's voice trailed off. I heard nothing beyond the shame in my own mind.

"No, it's just Nerf guns for my nephew's birthday." She punched the information into her computer. "These presents are late, though . . . I am never on time."

She let me talk, waiting until I was done to ask me when I wanted the presents to arrive.

I've already missed his birthday. Does it really matter when they get there? I laughed. Shaking myself out of a daze and into present reality. "So long as they get there, whatever rate is the cheapest." She ripped off the sticker and placed it on the box, covering the already glued down edges with more tape.

"Okay, it'll arrive in five to seven days." She handed me the receipt and circled the phone number I could call for a survey. "Next!"

I walked to my car, looking around, wondering if maybe Jade had waited for me, but her car was not in the parking lot. *Yeah, she's gone. That was the moment I prayed for?*

I climbed inside my car and closed the door, dissatisfied. I lay my head on the headrest and looked out the window. *I thought it would go differently. Am I nothing to her? Was I ever anything to her?* Maybe this reality check *was* good for me.

I embraced the ache in my chest, again. *Love, where are you? I thought I wanted this. . . . Oh love, come close.*

I turned my keys over and heard the engine start. I looked at the clock—almost five o'clock. And I thought of him: the one who was still waiting so patiently for me. The one who had never left me. The one who offered himself to me daily, with all his love and all his gentleness. The one who got up at night with me, vowing to fight the demons in my dreams. The one who had given me the freedom to leave.

I will not make you stay, Lindsey. He had said it, time and time again—the one who had only ever wanted me to choose him.

twenty-two

Finding Home

One of my favorite things to do after leaving Jen's home was to get lost on the country roads. Tennessee is a beautiful state, and despite how long I'd been living there, I never got over the beauty of the rolling hills and the acres of land and horses that I dreamt of one day owning myself.

Sometimes, though, I would feel guilty for making it out of my hometown and living in such a captivating place. I found it difficult to move past this guilt and fully embrace a new life when people I loved were dying back home.

I was on a road trip with Jonathan, visiting his family in Florida, when I found out my friend Keya had been shot dead. I'd sensed something was wrong before I even answered the phone—because the person who called hadn't touched based for a while. Something was obviously up. There was a season, right around this time, when people seemed to be dying in droves back home. Friends' dads were dying by suicide. Kids

I grew up in school with were killed by gang violence or bad drug deals. Childhood friends fell victim to meth addictions or were caught by the authorities. I came across the mug shot of an old friend and nearly threw up; I saw no spark left in her eyes, though she was once so full of life and personality.

When I heard the news about Keya, I detached from the pain of it. The reality of life back home was now just facts to me. *I'm not living there anymore. I don't have to feel this. That town is never going to change.* I had intentionally left this world behind, but people I cared about deeply were still stuck in a city I would have rather forgotten about. I was still facing so much in my marriage and actively trying to implement the healing tools I had learned in therapy. As such, the news of any new death was almost too much for my newly opened and vulnerable heart to carry.

However, as hard as I tried to forget the news, I couldn't escape the sadness. I looked up the most recent news article about Keya's death, which had been ruled a double homicide. Both she and her boyfriend were robbed and murdered in a home invasion. The paper called it "a violent death." I fixed my eyes on that sentence and remembered the seat we shared on the bus on our way to show choir events. I thought about how beautifully she could sing, and how we all asked her to sing for us when we'd hang out together. I remembered the way she wholeheartedly loved her mother—a single mom who, even though she struggled with a debilitating disease, showed up to every single event Keya was part of. That disease ended up taking her mom's life, leaving Keya without her best friend. I put my phone away, unable to read any more. *Well, she's with her mom now.* I didn't think of this dismissively, but as an effort to shove the grief aside. Where Keya had gone was far better than the place she had left.

It was so hard to reckon with the pain of losing another friend. But it didn't matter how far I wanted to separate myself from the loss; I held an invisible tether to the people back home that I didn't want to cut loose. I didn't drive back for the funeral. Now I wish I had.

Some losses, though, you cannot detach from. Two years after Keya passed, I got a text from my best friend. She'd seen on Facebook that my cousin Andrew had tried to take his own life. I was getting ready for a friend's wedding, curling my hair, when I first got her text. "Is Andrew okay?" I called her right away.

"What do you mean? I haven't heard anything." I started to panic.

"Oh my God, Lindsey. I thought you would have known." I hung up with her and called my mom. I won't ever be able to forget the helplessness in her voice as she broke the news to me.

I dropped the phone and started screaming. My daughter walked into the room and called out, "Mommy," as Jonathan ran in and swooped her up. I just kept repeating, "Andrew. He killed himself. He wasn't supposed to do this. We were in this together." We'd had numerous three a.m. conversations, when he'd call me after drinking with his buddies and break down in sobs when he realized just how lonely he was. Alcohol had made him the most honest—at least it seemed that way to me. I always took his call. I'd sit up in bed, turn the light on, and let Jonathan know it was Andrew. Jonathan would nod his head and place his hand on my arm before falling back asleep, to let me know I was not alone. But Andrew didn't call me this night.

My mom, knowing how devastated I was and how far away I was from my family, offered advice to make it through the night. "Go and try to enjoy the wedding, Lindsey." She knew how hard this was. "There is no decision to make yet. His mom and dad are there with him now. He's on a ventilator, but they are taking him off tonight."

"Wait, what? He's . . . he's not dead? Why are they taking him off so soon? They have to wait!" I panicked. *Oh God, no. There is still time then! God, we need a miracle.*

"He is gone, Lindsey. He will not recover from his brain damage."

I began to fight. "No, he's not! He is not gone!" I was angry that no one in my family believed in the possibility of a supernatural healing. It wasn't probable, but I believed it was possible. *Why can't they just wait!*

My mom let me cry. She was hurting too. "You can come home tomorrow, after we know more." She was as supportive and tender as she could be.

I went to the wedding with Jonathan. He held me tight on his arm, attuned to the grief I tried hard to put away for the night.

I watched my beautiful friend walk down the aisle as the

sun was setting, knowing this was the day she was starting a new life with an incredible man, surrounded by everyone who loved them. I snapped a picture of my friend in her dress and smiled as she walked past me, but my heart was gone, painfully aware that tomorrow, as she woke up next to her new groom, I would be on my way to Indiana to bury my cousin.

The next morning, Jonathan and I loaded up the car and headed north. He grabbed my hand and interlaced his fingers with mine. I turned my face toward him, laying my head on the headrest so I could look at him as he drove. He had loved Andrew, too, so I knew this was hard for him.

I watched him carefully and listened to him explain to our daughter why we could only stay at her grandparents' house for two nights. We had to get back to *our* home, he told her. I rested my eyes. *Our home.* I thought about how, in just a few days, we'd cross back into the state of Tennessee and I'd release a deep sigh of relief. *My refuge.*

After the funeral had ended, we lined up outside to hear the 21-gun salute that every fallen veteran gets. Though Andrew didn't die in active duty, his death was surely a result of war. I closed my eyes as I listened to the guns fire. Jonathan held me close, my two worlds now colliding. I realized I didn't have to face this alone anymore. He was with me here. His presence was calming. He was safe.

He is home.

twenty-three

Yellow Roses

I was outside, shovel in hand, breaking up the soil in front of our home. I sat on the porch steps to take a quick break. I admired the yellow rosebush I'd just bought. It was the ten-year anniversary of Lynsey's death and I wanted to plant new life in memory of her.

I'd been trying my hand at gardening and had recently torn up the years' worth of weeds that grew along the fence in our backyard. It was easy for me to tear apart what wasn't working anymore, but it wasn't as easy knowing what to do with a blank canvas.

Jonathan sent one of the kids—we had three of them by now—to bring me a glass of water. They ran off right after handing it to me; I knew that signaled they didn't want to be asked to help. Working in the yard was something only I liked to do. But I preferred it this way. There was something satisfying about the repetitiveness of digging in the soil, making a hole to plant the roots in.

My neighbor came outside and waved at me. She was joining me in a day of yard work. She and I had become great friends, and so had our daughters. I remembered back to the first time we met each other. We had just moved into this house. We were unpacking boxes in our kitchen when Jonathan and I heard a knock on our garage door.

That's a funny place to hear a knock, I thought.

Jonathan opened the door, and there were our new neighbors, coming over to say hello. They were so friendly and so casual. Jo had a flower crown in her hair, and I knew immediately that our daughters would be good friends. We tried to be neighborly, too: friendly when we rolled the trash cans to the edge of the driveway or checked the mail at the same time. We waved hello when we passed each other in the car and let our kids ride their bikes together.

But the friendship we developed was unique.

Not long after Jo and her husband introduced themselves, I watched an ambulance pull up to their house with its lights flashing and sirens on. I dropped what I was doing and ran over there, right through the front door, as if I'd known them for years. Maybe I was more comfortable doing so because they'd first come knocking on our garage door instead of our front door. This made me think they were unconventional in their ways and much more concerned with just being *neighborly* than complying with social standards.

I moved inside and saw Jo standing ahead of me. She had her hand over her mouth, covering it in disbelief. I looked to my left and noticed legs on the ground and the paramedics swirling around a girl who appeared no older than twenty. Jo looked at me and dropped her head as if she was giving up.

"She swallowed a bottle of pills," she said before her voice broke. I knew that was my call to move. I wrapped my arms around her while she cried into my shoulder, her head buried in her hands.

The only words I could muster were: "You're a good mother. This is not your fault. You're a good mother." I didn't know what else to say to a mother whose daughter wanted to go to sleep and not wake up. But I was a mother, so I knew how clever the voice of shame could be. I figured I'd start by exposing it to light.

I held Jo while the paramedics forced something into the body of her motionless daughter, causing her to throw up and breathe again. She vomited violently, releasing all signs of death from her body. She was fully alive. Her life was spared. But I knew it would take work for her to stay alive from here on out.

I hugged Jo tightly before she moved toward her daughter. That was the moment I decided to leave and let their family be together. I assured her I was right across the street if she needed anything at all. I exited her home and breathed a deep breath of renewal. After a shared experience like that, you aren't just neighborly anymore. You become deep friends.

Jo looked my way and commented on how pretty the yellow roses were. I thanked her and took a sip of water. She was always planting things in her yard, too, and giving me offshoots of plants she'd dug up. Sometimes we'd meet at the edge of our driveways and talk to each other, both with dirt on our knees, in our fingernails and hair. I set my glass down and went back to work.

I got down on my knees and scooped the dirt with my hands. I never wore gloves. I always liked the way the dirt felt in my fingers. The hole needed to be just a bit bigger than the base of the rosebush, so I used a hand shovel to cut through the soil. I grabbed the bush and wiggled the roots from the plastic container, careful to avoid the thorns that would poke me until I bled.

I set the plant in the hole and used my hands to spread the dirt evenly around it. When I got the ground level, I popped onto my feet and took a few steps back to look at it. The yellow roses reminded me of Lynsey. I have fewer memories of her now than I did back then. Time had a way of fading memories. But I'll never forget her smile, and probably not her hugs either. Having this rosebush planted just below the steps to my front door gave me a great excuse to think about her more often.

The kids ran around the front yard with the neighborhood friends they'd been playing with. "Mom, that's pretty!" said my oldest.

"Thank you. I planted it in memory of my friend Lynsey," I said.

My daughter stepped in close and whispered, somberly, "Oh, is that your friend who was killed?" She spoke of it like it was a secret, but I think she was trying to be respectful of my wishes not to mention it to her friends. She was always sensitive to this story, even though I never told her any of the details of it. I looked at her and nodded my head. This was a distant memory, but it felt even further away now that I had a daughter who was old enough to know about it. "She died ten years ago."

My daughter hugged me to show her compassion. Lynsey's date of death didn't make me as sad anymore—not because it wasn't a terribly heartbreaking day, but because when I saw her in my dreams, she looked exhilarated. I knew she was happy. Well cared for and wrapped wholly in love. So, I chose to start seeing her in a new light—one that reflected the beauty of who she was now, not the way she left this world.

Sometime later, after we had moved away from Nashville, we drove past the house with the yellow rosebush, and I was sad to think it wasn't ours anymore. But I saw that rosebush still there, having grown wild with yellow petals since I first planted it. We parked on the street just across from our old house and walked up the sidewalk to Jo's house. We knocked on the door, hoping to surprise her and her husband with a visit. We'd grown close, and it was hard not to see them as often as we used to. Our kids were all older now, but they played together as easily as they did when they were little. The girls went to a bedroom to do some painting, and our son followed along with them. Jo and her husband offered Jonathan and me a drink.

We sat down on their couch with our homemade limoncellos and caught up. They knew we'd moved back to Indiana, but it was Indianapolis we now called home—not the town I grew up in, thirty miles north of the city. They asked if we were settling in, and I was honest about the struggle.

"You know, I have family from your hometown," Jo said.

"Really? How have we never talked about this before?" I laughed, a bit shocked.

"I have no idea." Jo laughed too.

"What are their names? Watch, I probably know them!"

The world felt small. What were the odds, though, that I would actually know the relative she had in my hometown?

Jo sipped her drink and uttered a name—the name of a cousin who worked at the Christian college in my hometown.

And that was it. I felt all the blood leave my face. Jonathan, having not noticed, said, "Oh yeah, I bet Lindsey knows her! Or maybe an aunt of hers who used to work at the college."

They both looked at me, but I hesitated. "No, I—I don't

know her . . ." I took a long sip of my drink, wondering if the expression on my face told them I was lying.

I pulled out my phone and typed her cousin's name into the Facebook search bar. I thought I knew who she was, but I needed to make sure. I hoped I was wrong. Everyone else moved on in the conversation, and I was thankful because I would need some time to sit with this one if it was true. And then, I saw it: the name of her cousin and Jo as the mutual friend we shared.

Jo is related to the man who murdered Lynsey.

Jonathan and I collected the kids and said our goodbyes. I held it together because I wanted my friendship with Jo from the last several years to last beyond this new revelation. I didn't want to talk about it with her yet. I thought back on all my conversations with her and how I'd usually refer to Lynsey as "my friend who was killed," never actually using her name.

Did I even tell her it was a murder?

I started to question how much of this story I'd told Jo. I'd shared pieces of my life with her, especially after the scare with her oldest daughter. Had I never mentioned *this*?

I shut the car door, and Jonathan immediately read my body language. "What's the matter?" he asked.

How do I even say this? It would be the first time I'd said it out loud. I was still in shock.

"Babe . . . Jo's cousin's son murdered Lynsey."

Jonathan gasped. A minute of silence passed as we both wrapped our minds around this. Then a memory returned to me. "The first and last time I ever saw Jo's cousin was the day she sat in court, watching her son be led away in cuffs with a life sentence. It was a death for her that day too."

We pulled out of Jo's driveway and passed the rosebush again. This totem left in the front yard of my old house now had new meaning. Unless intentionally dug up, the flowers would remain there for years to come. And I had to wonder if my idea to plant these yellow roses in Tennessee—where the story of redemption was still playing out—was initially God's idea or Lynsey's.

What I couldn't get past were two very tangible realities. One, that no matter how far I run, I can never outrun the life attached to me—every moment from the time I took my very first breath to the day I will take my last, and every single heartache and joy in between. My story is mine, and it will always travel with me. I could see my story as shackles, or I could call it shoes. Either way, it'll carry me. And two, the story isn't finished. There is still healing to come, soil to dig, seeds to bury, roses to bloom.

It had been a week since I'd discovered Jo's ties to Lynsey, and I was ready to call and tell her I'd lied—that I actually knew who her cousin was. After this revelation, I found God to be terribly detailed. I no longer passed things off as coincidence, but I'd search for meaning. I wouldn't always find what I went looking for, but I believed it would eventually be found.

I did a quick Google search on the symbolism of yellow

roses. My phone loaded the page, which said, "Yellow roses symbolize friendship." *Of course that's what they mean.* A reminder that relationships are precious and complicated and beautiful—worthy to be nurtured and cherished.

I dialed Jo.

twenty-four

The Affair

Oh God, oh God, this hurts so bad. I took his phone, the one I held in my hands, and threw it across the room, hoping to smash it. *I cannot unsee what I've seen.* I was breathing but couldn't catch my breath. I beat my fists into the pillows on my bed, shuffling through the blankets in a rampage until the weight of the news settled on me and I felt myself drop to the ground. I was crying so hard I expected a child to come banging on my bedroom door.

I spotted Jonathan's boots on the floor—the really nice ones he'd often wear on our date nights. I walked over and picked them up. *I'm throwing these away.* Then I grabbed his favorite hats, favorite jeans, and favorite shirts, piling them all in my arms to take them to the trash. *If he wore them out with me, then he wore them out with her.*

I walked past Jonathan, who sat on the couch—barely able to move from the pain he was facing himself. He looked up at me, his clothes in my hands, and asked if I could just stop for a moment and talk. But I was in a rage, and I didn't want to stop. I wanted to get rid of every single item he owned that made him think of her. I opened the door with one hand, still balancing the clothes in my arms, and walked myself out to the trash can in our garage. I opened the lid and threw everything in.

There's still more. I want to throw away every single thing he loves.

I raced back inside and grabbed all our expensive liquor and craft beer, not forgetting to grab his favorite whiskey glasses before heading out for another dumpster drop. I threw it all in the bin, feeling only slightly satisfied at the sound of the glass shattering from the force; I needed it to be a whole lot louder than it was to match the rage inside of me.

I walked back inside, breathing heavy as if I'd been on a sprint. I stomped over to the couch. "You still have not told me the whole truth." I waited, giving him only a quick chance to respond before I'd tell him how I knew with certainty that he was still hiding something.

"I've told you everything," he lied.

"No, you haven't. I hacked your phone. I've seen everything."

His countenance dropped.

"If you don't tell me every single detail about her, I will leave you. I swear to you, Jonathan. Everything will be over."

It was just three days before our twelfth wedding anniversary, and I had no idea that in just a few days I'd discover that Jonathan had been entertaining a life with someone else. My curiosity got the best of me while we were drinking a bottle of wine one evening, working on a puzzle after our kids went to bed. I was processing a relationship of mine that had just ended—an emotional affair that had distanced me not just from my husband but from my entire family. I wanted her to feel the same way about me as I did about her, but she didn't. When I told her how I was really feeling, and how I needed to end our friendship, she told me to never contact her again. It wasn't a pretty goodbye, by any means, but it was necessary.

I took a sip of wine and exchanged a smile with Jonathan. *How can he continue loving me when I haven't always chosen him?*

I searched for another puzzle piece, flipping over the ones that were still facedown. "Jonathan . . ." I was curious at this point, having never noticed my husband dealing with an underlying issue like porn or fantasizing about being with other women. Some of our close friends had recently entered SA (Sexaholics Anonymous) for addiction to pornography, and it just seemed like Jonathan was too perfect—like there was nothing he struggled with outside of the normal emotional distress of being an adult. "Have you ever really struggled with, like, other women?" I couldn't come up with a smoother way to ask him. It felt silly to even say it aloud. He moved around in his seat a little bit, adjusting to reach for another puzzle piece. I didn't take my eyes off him, studying him like an investigator looking for clues.

Our dog began to whine at his side. Her cry was so loud that it pulled all our focus to her. Jonathan pushed out of his chair. "Gosh, I can't take it. I have to let her outside." He was clearly agitated as he motioned for the dog to go outside. I lowered my eyes as he walked back in, not wanting him to feel like I was searching for something.

I'd been known to play private investigator before, reading his text messages to make sure he wasn't hiding something. He sat down and looked at me. "I mean, of course I struggle. I'm human."

His answer made me nervous. *That feels like a slide right out of the conversation.* But as he probably already knew from being with me for over a decade, I wasn't going to let it go that easily.

"Okay, but what does that even mean?" I pried harder. I was *definitely* looking for something now, bracing myself for the moment I'd learn my husband was harboring a secret porn addiction. *We can handle this. It's going to be fine*, I reassured myself. He shifted again in his seat, leaning back as he put his hands in his lap, the puzzle now forgotten. "Okay, yeah, I guess I could share with you a time I struggled with another woman."

Deep breath, Lindsey. I stayed as calm and gentle as I could. I knew he would shut down if I got angry.

He told me her name. I didn't flinch. *How can I be upset with him when I've done the same thing to him?* "I met her at a bar when Clay and I hung out." He continued, knowing I was asking for more but not saying a single word. "She was our bartender, and we started talking."

I interrupted him, knowing he wasn't finished sharing yet. "What did you talk about?" I wanted to know every word of their conversation. I was already drawing up conclusions—or worst-case scenarios—that they'd decided on the date when he'd leave me to be with her. I had even trailed so far off path that I was already wondering if our kids would love her more than they loved me. But I was still playing it cool, trying not to show him my cards just yet.

"Mainly, we talked about our past church hurt."

Oh, okay. That's not too bad. So, he found a woman attractive and they connected over past pain. I get it.

"But I started to get a little more curious about her and looked her up on Instagram, and then we started talking that way. But once I realized I didn't want to talk to her anymore, I ended it."

I nodded my head slowly, then looked back at the puzzle. I searched for a piece as if I cared to keep finding the right fit, but I was only trying to stay calm and rein in my thoughts before my assumptions caused me to spiral. "Well, thanks for telling me," I told him.

It wasn't until the next morning that I asked him for the name of the bar. He hesitated to tell me, probably guessing what would come next: the social media stalking. He was exactly right. From the first picture I saw of her, I felt pain in my stomach, and I knew without a doubt: *There's more to the story here.*

I promised to not bug him again while he was at work. Surely I could wait patiently until he got home to ask him more questions. It was only ten in the morning, but I was already *deep* into my imagination at what could have happened between them. More accurately, after noticing the way she carried herself for the world to see, I wondered what *she* had asked of him. Even so, I wanted to believe the best of my husband.

By two o'clock, I hadn't eaten a thing all day. I texted him: "I looked her up. I know who she is. I am sick. Can you please come home?"

He waited only a few minutes and responded: "I'll pack up here in five."

I paced every square inch of our fifteen-hundred-square-foot ranch home. I walked back and forth, from the back bedroom to the kitchen, and then did it all over again. My mind was in the ring, a boxing match between trust and doubt.

I am blowing this out of proportion.

Something happened. I can feel it.

Oh no. I don't want to face this.

Calm down, Lindsey. He would never cheat on you.

God, please help. Please, please help.

He pulled into the driveway, and I took a seat on the couch. Our youngest child was up from her nap and playing with her toys on the living room rug. When he walked in, I felt as though I would throw up. He looked that way too. I walked over to him and gave him a hug. *It's going to be okay.*

"Jonathan, there is more you're not telling me. I can feel it, babe." I was patient, but growing desperate for the truth.

He sat down on the couch, clearly defeated, like he was in his own boxing ring of inner dialogue. He sighed and looked into my eyes. I noticed the weight behind his.

He's cheated on me. I can see it all over him.

The next twenty-four hours were the worst. I searched for answers. Pried. Asking him the same questions over and over until I'd out find the truth—me never getting all the details at once like I needed. Each new confession tore my heart apart a little more, having never believed I'd experience a pain like this one.

Slowly, I came to grips with another woman in the picture who had taken my place.

"When did it start?" I asked, forgetting to even ask how long ago it was.

"I ended things almost a year ago."

A whole year has gone by? Oh my God, he has been hiding for an entire year?

I paced the house again, running through all the memories we shared over the past year. Was the man I shared them with a complete fraud?

A whole year?

I could not understand how he'd kept this in for so long. "Did you tell *anyone*?"

He shook his head no. I just stared at him sitting still on the couch like he was afraid of adding more movement to my already anxious pacing.

My gut told me there was still more. "You're still not telling me everything."

He sighed, exhausted. "Lindsey, I've told you everything you need to know."

I laughed in mockery, because he'd already said that five

other times—*before* telling me more he hadn't told me. "Well, that's not good enough. Give me your phone."

He didn't resist and handed it to me. I walked to the back bedroom as the bus pulled up and dropped off our two older kids from school. I locked our door, opened his phone, and opened every single social media account he possessed. I searched every message, every comment. *Why am I not finding her?* And it occurred to me what he'd already mentioned—the night we worked on the puzzle together—that he'd blocked her so she wouldn't try to reach out to him again. So, I unblocked her, went to their messages, and watched the conversations roll across the screen. Then I fell apart.

I stormed back out into the living room.

"If you don't tell me every single detail about her, I will leave you. I swear to you, Jonathan. Everything will be over."

Our oldest daughter walked into the room, sensing something was terribly wrong. I looked over at her, timidly interrupting us. *She doesn't deserve this. I am so sorry she has witnessed this.* "Is everyone okay?" she asked.

"It's okay, everything will be okay. Daddy hurt Mommy, but everything is going to be okay."

She looked at her dad. "What?" She started to panic, and I realized my words connected to a *physical* hurt in her mind.

"Oh, no, he just did something that hurt my feelings." I

couldn't even finish the sentence without crying. How could one explain this to their child without breaking them too?

Jonathan whispered, "I'm so sorry. I'm just so sorry," before breaking down himself.

I was more concerned for our children than I was for his feelings. Our daughter walked over to her baby sister and lifted her into her arms, giving her a kiss on the forehead. I assured her that everything would be all right. She took her baby sister into her bedroom to play and invited her younger brother to join them too, who had been in his room building Legos. Our arguing lasted well into the evening, breaking only to let our children eat their dinner without hearing the strife.

After dinner, I walked the kids back into their older sister's room, where she'd read them a book and keep them occupied. "I'll be in to tuck you all in soon, okay?" I gently shut their bedroom door behind me, but I never made it back to tuck them into bed. The task had fallen on our oldest instead.

I walked back into the living room in a frantic search for my phone. I couldn't face my husband anymore. I needed to call someone—anyone. I needed to know I wasn't alone. *Where the hell is it?* I searched the countertops, my bedroom, and underneath the couch, growing more frustrated that I still hadn't found it.

"My God! Where is my phone?" I shouted. Jonathan reached underneath the throw blanket that I had been curled up underneath earlier in the day, after texting him to come home from work. He offered the phone to me, and I snatched it from his grasp, struggling to find one emotion to settle on as I moved between rage and helplessness. I scrolled through the running list of names stored in my phone and landed on one: Jen's mobile.

"Can I call you? Jonathan's cheated on me," I typed.

She texted back almost immediately. "Oh Linds, yes, you can call now." It'd been ten years since I sat on the love seat in Jen's home, but we had remained friends. I knew, without a doubt, that she was as willing now as she was back then to pick up the phone and talk me off the ledge.

I locked myself inside our car and sat in the driveway. I found the key, started the car, and considered driving to the bar. Jen picked up on the first ring, and I did not hide my anger.

"I'm going to kill her, Jen. I'm going to kill her." She tried to settle me down by asking me some questions, causing my brain to divert its attention from driving to the bar and hurting this girl to processing the details with her.

"Linds, if you drive to that bar, I am going to drive there too," she said. "Think about your family—and your children. You hurt this woman, and you will go to jail."

I let out a loud cry, aware there was absolutely *nothing* I could do to relieve the pain I felt. "I can't believe he would do this, Jen. I never thought he was capable of this."

It just hurts so bad. As Jen and I talked on the phone, she tended to my broken heart the best she could. But rather than talking to me as a therapist would, she spoke to me as a friend. I admired her attentiveness, even now, and felt loved by the sadness I heard in her voice as she offered empathy at my news.

I walked back inside and the house was dark. I noticed the relief in Jonathan's voice when he told me he was so afraid I would end up doing something I couldn't take back. I can only imagine how beat up I must have looked, having just let out my rage on the car steering wheel. My eyes still burned from the tears.

"I'm going to bed," I told Jonathan. *I can't care any more tonight.*

"Do you want me to sleep out here?"

I stopped in my tracks and almost laughed out loud. *Of course I want you to sleep as far away from me as possible. I don't want to look at you or touch you or hear you breathe.*

But was that really what I wanted? I was hurting, but he had been my person, which doesn't just change overnight. Still standing in the hallway, never turning around to face him, I thought about his question. "I don't care where you sleep," I blurted out. But that was a lie. I did care. As much as he'd hurt me, I wanted him closer to me than ever. I wanted him to hold me. He was the only one I'd ever trusted with my heavy heart. I shut the door to our room and climbed into bed.

Five minutes later, I heard him enter our room. I did not look at him but closed my eyes like I was asleep. When he slid into bed, trying very hard to not disturb me, I opened my eyes and saw his body at the very edge of the bed. He cried quietly. For the first time that night, my heart moved toward forgiveness.

I didn't move. *He wants to disappear. I know the shame he feels.* I closed my eyes, feeling the pressing of a spirit of love inside of me, asking me to move closer to my husband. *I do not want to do this. I do not want to give him any bit of my affection. He does not deserve any of my love right now.* But he did. And I remembered the moments he'd loved me back to life—moments when I didn't deserve it. The moments he stayed patient with me when my heart was attached to someone else. I reached out my arm and touched his shoulder. He began to cry louder.

"Lindsey, I am so sorry I've hurt you."

I propped myself up in the bed, and he turned over to face me. I reached out my arms and hugged him to my chest, where he could lie and cry for as long as he needed.

The next morning, our emotions were still raw, but the rage had passed. I felt a lull of sadness too. He was sitting on the couch watching soccer with our son when I walked out. "Jonathan, can I talk to you for just a second?"

He told our son he'd be right back, then came into the bedroom with me. I cried again, just from looking at him. He cried again too. It was so hard to *not* cry when we faced each other. But I had not asked him to come back into the room so we could cry together. I had clarity on what I needed from him to move forward. I wiped my tears and took his hands in mine, still suspecting there were more details he hadn't disclosed.

"You have until tomorrow at three p.m. to tell me absolutely everything, and I will not leave you. Everything. But if you lie to me again, our marriage will end."

Maybe it was the controlled authority in my tone or the fact that I'd calmed down in my requests, but he nodded his head in agreement. "Okay. I will tell you everything then."

The next day at three, we sat down facing each other. My neighbor had offered to take our kids for the day. He pulled out a letter he'd written. "It was easier for me to write everything down. But I need to speak it, so I'm going to read it to you," he said.

I placed a small trash can beside me in case I needed to throw up. He opened the letter and began to read it. And I knew after that moment: *that's everything.*

twenty-five

A New Israel

The road was lined with signs that read: "Danger! Land mines." We kept straight on the dirt road, traveling a far distance to the site where Jesus was baptized. I noticed that the road to baptism was not pristine, with paved sidewalks and nicely manicured lawns on either side. It was dusty and dangerous—with a constant threat of explosion on either side of us. I wondered if ever again I'd be so close to the ground beneath me blowing up.

I knew we were getting close when I saw a building, or more like an outdoor pavilion, with nicely constructed common areas built around the holy river—a spot providing sideline views, like baptism was a spectator sport. You could stand above and watch the spiritually dead come to life, or you could climb a few steps down and be right in the action.

Our driver pulled over when we were clear of the mines and parked the bus. The people began to stir, stretching their legs, moving around to try and get a better view of the surrounding space. We'd been staring at fields of land mines, completely empty except for a few cows that roamed freely—and naïvely.

We stepped off the bus, and I saw locker rooms stocked with white bathrobes should we want to change into something holier than the yoga pants and sweaty T-shirts everyone had worn to sightsee in the desert. I took note of the individual showers for after a baptism, for cleaning up before stepping into the gift shop that sold "Holy Jordan River Water."

We approached a guard with a large gun, and I smiled at her. She looked like she'd just graduated from high school. We had been told not to cross the IDF (Israeli Defense Force), which I noted once we arrived at the airport in Tel Aviv. I had watched a beautiful Israeli woman, no older than nineteen, give our ex-military, muscleman guide a difficult time, taking his passport and not giving him any information regarding if or when he might get it back. If they hadn't let *him* in the country, none of us would have made it. It had taken thirty minutes of interrogation before they let him in.

At the airport, I had patiently waited for my turn to be called to the security checkpoint. Surely she'd give the rest of us a hard time too. I prepared myself. The guard called Jonathan and me up together, and I walked a step behind him. I handed her my passport. She studied my ID and then studied my face. "Smile," she said very directly. So, with awkwardness, I turned my lips up and showed her my teeth. "You're prettier now than you are in your picture."

I chuckled, unable to tell if she was flirting with me or

calling out how bad my ID picture was. "Thank you," I said. Then a smile came more naturally.

She closed my passport and winked at me. "Welcome to Israel."

I noted: *If there is ever a problem, run to the IDF women first.* They were no-nonsense, solid as rocks, and unafraid of threats. By now, toward the end of our trip, I'd gotten used to the loaded rifles on the shoulders of every guard—that is, every nineteen-year-old kid.

Outside the bus and near the river, I struggled to take it all in—where I was and the significance in front of me. It was hard to believe that this was the river, thousands of years ago, where Jesus himself first modeled death and new life. I looked ahead and saw the steps that led to the river. Anyone who wanted to be baptized was encouraged to change into a swimsuit, but I'd left my clothes on. I was ready to immerse myself in the river. I wanted to feel the rush of water flowing over me as my hair swirled in the wake of my body being pushed under. I didn't want an experience; I wanted a baptism.

My husband followed me to the top of the stairs. I was ready to see this river. My eyes widened in shock. It was the dirtiest water I'd ever seen. It was cloudy and brown, like a deep mud puddle. I started to second-guess this decision. Was this water even safe to get in? I feared putting my toe in, let alone dunking my whole body under.

I weighed the options of a baptism versus a stomach illness. I'd heard how the river had recently been shut down because it failed to pass a basic sanitation test, but I figured they'd have bleached it since then—like a pool. In the two minutes it took the rest of my group to catch up to where we stood, I had gone over every reason why this was a bad idea. *You're just a tourist. You don't need this. You were baptized when you were a kid. The water's dirty. It's unsafe. Is it* really *worth it if you're almost guaranteed to get sick?* I offered an unsure half-smile to my husband. We walked down the stairs together, but by the time I came face-to-face with the river, I'd already made my decision.

Leaning in close to Jonathan, I asked, "Will you baptize me?"

Only twenty of us were on this trip, which was a significantly smaller tour group compared to the large church groups that I'd seen tour Israel together. During our time together, the small crew had bonded. My husband was hired to shoot video of the entire trip, so the moments where he was without a large, expensive camera on his shoulder were rare. He looked down at me and smiled that cute but slightly uncomfortable smile I knew so well—when he was choosing to do something out of love, not necessarily because he wanted to.

"Yes," he said.

I knew he wasn't prepared to get in the water, but true to his nature—always willing to go to the ends of the earth for me—he set his camera down, took off his shoes, and grabbed my hand. In a moment of sheer intimacy, everyone in our group quieted and watched us step into the muddy water. The intensity of that moment made it feel as though they'd been on our journey with us the whole time—a journey filled with its own land mines, stone-faced guards, and disappointment. Oh, the disappointment. A wife who could never give her full heart, having chased the fantasy of what life would look and feel like with someone else, who had spoken more about divorce than restoration, who was so coldhearted toward her husband that she rejected his love more times than she accepted it. A husband who had fought for his wife but given into the temptation of attention from another woman, whose affection, on the surface, seemed more simple and certain. But this moment felt truly redemptive.

Here I was. Here he was. Standing in this filthy water. One before God.

I leaned into his chest and whispered to him, "I'm nervous." And I could tell he was a little too. I was fully clothed, but I felt naked in front of him and all these people around us. He held my back with his right hand as he laid his left hand on my shoulder. I couldn't tell if the slight tremble was coming from my adrenaline or his hands. He spoke quietly to me, whispering in my ear so the others couldn't hear, of how far we'd come and how he was happy to still be standing next to me. There was emotion behind his eyes, and I remembered back to those same eyes on our wedding day. Full of loyalty, and even fuller of hope. It was now just him and me. This holy moment between us. Us interlocking with the divine person himself, a three-corded strand.

"Lindsey," he said. But I heard: *my beloved.* "I baptize you in the name of the Father, of the Son, and of the Holy Spirit."

He held the weight of my body as he leaned me back, pushing me all the way under the water, and I trusted that he wouldn't leave me there. He didn't want me to stay underwater—he'd *never* wanted me to stay underwater. With more strength now—carrying not only the weight of his bride but also the weight of the water above her—he used his power to lift a new body, a living body, up from the grave that once held her. I felt the dry desert air hit my wet face and let go of my tightly held breath, inhaling new life deep into my lungs. I wiped my eyes and curled my wet, muddy body into the chest of my husband. I tucked my arms between us as he held me. I didn't want to leave this water.

The river. The muddy waters. The rush of healing. The scattering of disappointments. The moment I submerged myself in the same dirty water that thousands had submerged themselves in before me—as though we were all of the same dirt, the same sin, being washed in the same stain-colored river, hoping to be made clean.

The water I saw flowing through the Jordan River was filthy, but maybe what we see as filthy, God sees as crystal clear. And maybe, if we could just enter that water, we'd become less afraid of the muck.

Maybe healing requires us to sink down into the depths of our own filth, trusting that the strong hand on our back has the ability to lift us up out of it. But what if we refuse to enter the water? How devastating to remain a bystander, only ever observing someone else's deliverance and never coming fully to our own.

Entering the water requires a nakedness before God, where one look at our vulnerable bodies causes us to seek a hiding place; but we are the ones who seek to be hidden. Our perception is limited, seeing only the shame that covers us, while God only ever sees our infinite beauty—our belonging.

My freedom lay in that dirty water. Entering the muck of my own pain and discomfort, and facing my own vulnerability, was the only real fear I had to face. And I asked myself: *What if the road paved with dirt—lined with land mines—was always the safest road for me?* Everything in me whispered, *You might die out here*—yet death was my only way to enter new life.

In the grave, beneath the weight of the water, a holy moment took me while my old identity left me. The old identity told me I had to hide, that I'd be rejected if I was known, that I was unforgivable and unworthy of love. The identity that said I'd never be good enough—now was gone. She died that day, in the Jordan River—but she rose again, a new woman.

twenty-six

The Surrender

Our kids ran to get their shoes from the basket I kept in the entryway. I told them we were taking a family walk—which actually meant Jonathan and I would walk while the kids rode their bikes. We wanted to catch the last moments of a sun setting over the trees in our neighborhood, and if we had time before it got too dark, we'd end our walk at the lake just across the street from our home.

It had been two years since I found out about his affair, three years since he was with her. Though I thought about it sometimes, it didn't hold space in my memory the way it first did. And I don't think it held much space in his memory either. Whenever I'd bring it up, sifting through the details again like I was on an endless search to find a new detail he missed, he'd get uncomfortable when I spoke her name. It was a memory he hoped to forget, though I told him she would always be a part of a greater story no matter how hard he tried to remove her from it.

Since the day when the truth finally came out, I experienced my marriage differently. We both became very aware of our own limitations—mine no longer being the only focus. And maybe that was the problem all along: that we only ever spent time on what *I* was feeling, neglecting the simple fact that my husband was also a being who desired to be wanted and chosen. We both now understood we were only ever just one decision away from tearing it all right down again. Maybe next time we'd never be able to repair it. But I hoped we would never find out.

Though I believed I knew everything about his past, and he believed he knew everything about mine, the sobering reality remained that we both may never truly know all the details. I had grown more comfortable with the unknowns. I stopped searching for answers—not regarding his affair, but for answers to my own personal questions. The questions that still presented themselves on the days my loneliness couldn't be filled by my husband. And yet, I still wondered, *Will we ever be truly fulfilled this side of heaven?* I don't know the answer to that, but I know one thing: my own personal fulfillment feels like an impossible responsibility to lay on someone else.

We were both ready to move forward, to continue building the life we'd spent years laying the foundation for, brick by brick. This did not mean forgetting the past, but rather letting it remain there, in the past. We had to stand before the truth that though we both will always fall terribly short of earning the love we desired, we were both still worthy of it—unconditionally.

I reached for the pink aluminum-lined wineglass that read "Mom Juice." The kids had gotten it for me the previous Mother's Day, and I filled it to the top with Cabernet. "You taking a to-go glass?" Jonathan asked.

"You know it." I chuckled. *Surely this glass will be discreet enough for our neighbors.* I laughed as I put the lid on my silly attempt to nonchalantly hide my alcohol. Now that we had three children, these were the only date nights Jonathan and I got. I was going to take advantage of every minute.

Our youngest was crying by the shoe bin. Her older siblings had already laced up and run outside, leaving her struggling to get her shoes on the correct feet. Jonathan walked over to see if he could help. I noticed his attentiveness to her needs, the same attentiveness he had always given mine. He was patient. Gentle. Slow to get frustrated even when she yelled, "Daddy, I got it!" He removed his hands and let her try, fail, and try again.

She jumped to her feet and rushed outside to grab her tricycle. It was faster for her to keep up if she rode next to us while we walked. I handed Jonathan his own to-go wineglass of Cabernet on his way out. He tapped my glass with his to cheers, then came in for a kiss on my cheek. I tilted my face toward his, anticipating his kiss.

"Well, let's go!" I said, faking a smile for the both of us, pretending this "date night family walk" would be more relaxing than it typically proved to be. No matter how many times

I hoped our family walks around the block could be enjoyed without complaints about tired legs and hunger pangs, we never made it too far until the first kid chimed in—pushing the first domino over until each child was whining.

"You guys, we just left our driveway!" I'd say to them, annoyed. So, I'd just roll my eyes and sip my wine. *Maybe this is why I poured a to-go glass.* They knew I loved them, but they sure knew how to get under my skin.

As I was questioning yet again why we even bother with family walks, Jonathan said, "Because once we all get outside and get moving, we're better for it in the end." He was right. Midway through, when we got into the flow of movement, our tired legs would wake up and a fleet of endorphins would subdue any acute hunger pangs. I found the same technique to be useful in areas of my life that didn't pertain to physical exercise.

My son took off on his bike and raced his oldest sister. Our youngest peddled as fast as her little legs could go, barely keeping up with her dad and me as we walked by her side. Still, she was determined as ever to catch her big brother.

Our son made it around the first block and sped past us. He let go of one handlebar and stuck his right arm out, and I knew he was about to release his other hand too. *Please don't fall. Please don't fall.* I waited for the moment he'd lose his balance, just as I'm always bracing for the moment of catastrophe. But then I thought: *What if he lets go and he doesn't fall?*

My mind challenged my subconscious thoughts. Jonathan, seemingly in tune with my general anxiety, took my hand and held it tight, as if saying, *He'll be fine.* I moved my fingers through his and squeezed his hand back. I raised the glass to my lips and took a long, slow sip of my wine as we watched our son drop the other arm. Together, we heard the echo of his cheer as he flew down the only hill in our neighborhood.

I looked down at our three-year-old, who had also dropped her hands from the handlebars. With her arms down by her side, she wiggled right to left, perhaps thinking this movement would propel her faster than her actual legs. I nudged Jonathan to notice. How cute that she was mimicking her big brother.

My oldest rode up behind us, trying to catch her breath. "Can we go to the lake? I'm not going to go catch him again." She motioned her hand in a "forget him" sense, talking about her brother. He was in his own world, riding too fast for anyone to keep up.

I looked at Jonathan in response to her question. We'd have to cross a busy street to get to the bridge. But one road was all that separated us from the body of water I have always found solace in. "I'm up for going," I told him.

We put the bikes back in the garage and grabbed our dog to take with us. The kids argued over who could hold the leash before I told them it would be me who walked him. *Why do they have to argue about everything?* We walked to the end of the neighborhood, and I took our toddler's hand as we crossed the busy street. The kids ran along the sidewalk, and I took a deep, cleansing breath as we approached the pedestrian bridge built just above the water. The closer I got to the water, the more my mind relaxed.

The kids sat on a bench as Jonathan and I stood against the

wooden slats that kept us from the lake itself. The girls looked over the edge for turtles, and our son pointed out a fishing boat. "Dad, can we get one of those?" he asked. Our son loved the water as much as me. The dog sat at my feet, something we'd been working on in his puppy classes together, and I gave him a scratch on his head. He'd been such a gift to me over the past year, with an exceeding ability to comfort me through days of depression like no other dog had done before.

Jonathan put his arm around me as we watched the sun cast her last rays on the water that rippled into the bank below our feet.

I lifted my eyes up to the sky again. The clouds had parted, still flirting with the sun, and I was once again taken by the dance.

I fixed my gaze on the water. *I have made it back here. My place of rest when I am weak.*

I have found me.

I looked at Jonathan, my beautiful husband. I used to struggle to breathe when he moved in close. Now, I found safety in his arms. I used to panic at night, when it was time for bed, even though he'd assure me he had no expectations. Now, I looked forward to sleeping soundly, cuddled up, with him as my nook. He was patient with me when my heart was unattainable, when I could not give it to him in full, when I was lost in ache, when I guarded it at all costs because all the breaking and mending was still so damn fresh. He knew every single complicated detail of my heart, and not a single part of me was unwelcomed. His unconditional love changed me.

We're still learning the true meaning of a marriage. Every single day we wake up, we have a choice to make. We can choose each other or we cannot. Because we are never promised tomorrow, we are not bound in shackles to this commitment we've made to each other. But in this very breath, with the water and the world before us, I chose him and he chose me.

I've quit searching for answers. Maybe there are none. Maybe instead there is only joy and sadness, fear and courage. Maybe there are only choices. Successes and failures. Growth. I quit trying to numb the ache. Instead, I've learned to welcome it like a friend. A friend who pulls me back to the water, back to God, back to my husband, and back to myself. She is one of my greatest teachers, reminding me that I am only human, yet with a resilient human heart.

The sun pushed her way through one last time, as the clouds parted in reverence. I raised my arm to shelter my eyes. It was all so bright, but I welcomed the warmth on my face.

I am home.

Acknowledgments

Firstly, to my Jesus, your love is the reason I've kept breathing.

Mom and Dad, thank you for keeping our home a refuge. No matter what happened outside, I felt safe laying my head down at night. To my sister and brother, I am undeniably grateful for the both of you. I love you and your families deeply.

To my in-laws, you have witnessed my relationship with Jonathan over the years, and I can only imagine that it is your prayers that have carried us.

To my oldest girlfriends, you raised me. You taught me the weighted, honorable responsibility of being a loyal friend. I am who I am today because of you.

To Jill, thank you for carrying me on your back through the choppy waves of the Gulf of Mexico and for holding the zipper down on our tent when the neighborhood boys tried to scare us in the middle of the night. You've always managed to keep me protected one way or another.

To Elise Maurine, when the church tried to rip Jesus away from me, it was you he used to hold me tight. I am the most free when I am with you. (To Elise's parents, Rob and Lisa, I still owe you a lifetime of bagels and the confession that one time, while you were outside doing yard work, I snuck into your house so I could visit Elise while she was grounded.)

To Jen Otero, you took me in like family, let me invade your home with my angst and tears, and promised me I wasn't alone. Thank you for your unconditional love.

To Meg Kandros and Dane Anthony, thank you for walking the road of recovery with Jonathan and me.

To Bryan, Jess, Lindsay, Janet, Emily, Claire, Lauren, Mark, Tara, and Jamie—and all of our To Write Love on Her Arms family: You were the reprieve Jonathan and I needed during a wild, exhausting time. Thank you for loving us and making fourteen months of life in Florida exceptionally fun.

My dear editor-turned-friend, Lauren Langston Stewart, the level of vulnerability it takes to work on your life story with someone else is deep. From our first official meeting, you proved not only to be trustworthy in holding this space with me, but you understood my story on a level others have not. Your genuine encouragement and unparalleled expertise breathed new life into this book, and I will never tire of telling you how grateful I am for you.

To Matt West, Jocelyn Bailey, and the entire team at Dexterity Books, your integrity is evident. You elevate people over profit, and your goal to uphold this while running a business in a competitive market is what makes me especially proud to be a part of this family. I'm very grateful for a team who is fighting to get stories like mine told.

To Mick Silva and Nicole Edwards, you were the first editorial eyes on this memoir, long before I really knew what I needed to say. Thank you for your wisdom and guidance in leading me to write the best story I could.

To the irreplaceable friends I gained in Nashville, who cared most about loving me in my truest self and not putting up with any facade: Leslie Jordan, Ellie Greer, Stephanie Skipper, Dani Elliott, Emily Layton, Annie Agin, Betsy Boyer, Christina Griffith-Kurth, Renee Olson, Miranda Burnett, Cait Butcher, Becki Devries, Shelly Griffin, Hannah Smith Martin, Claire Tyner White, Megan Nikolayenko, Earnestine Sangster, Sarah Holihan, Dallas Atkinson, Jennifer Cooke, Jeanne Goskie, Tiffany Long, Becky Peterson, Mitch Goskie, Juan Otero, Andy Peterson, and Adam Agin.

To my kids. You were the first reason I found worthy of seeking help. You saved my life, but you do not carry the responsibility to keep saving it; I'll take it from here. You have every permission to be kids. And when you find yourself feeling lost, remember that you are tethered to me, and I will find you. You are never alone.

Lastly, to Jonathan. When waves of depression came to take me under, you swam out for me. You lifted me onto your board and paddled me back to shore, every single time. It was you who rubbed my back when I was lost in emptiness, you who told me life was still worth fighting for when my thoughts went dark, you who were endlessly patient during the triggers of past trauma. When people didn't understand our relationship, or why you held on, you stayed. It's obvious I would have no worthwhile story to tell if you were not a part of it. My life *is* you. I choose you.

About the Author

Lindsey Frazier is an author, a poet, and an advocate. Her writing style is a reflection of the way she lives: full of fierce, unapologetic love and hard-learned truths. She has spent the last decade of her life advocating for those on the margins, from her work in a day center for the homeless to becoming a certified Court Appointed Special Advocate (CASA) and a Victims of Violent Crime Assistant in the local prosecutors' office. Her conviction to embrace others through an active love is what keeps her awake at night.

Oh Love, Come Close is Lindsey's first memoir, but you can find her poetry in *Nashville Poets Quarterly* and *The Fold*, both local to Nashville, Tennessee, where she spent fifteen years of her life before returning to her home state of Indiana in 2020. In 2021 she won AAF Nashville's Co-Copywriter of the Year for a piece titled "Create More" that she coauthored with her husband, Jonathan. Her seven-day devotional, "Oh Love, Come Close: Seven Paths to Healing and Finding Freedom in Christ"—which has over ten thousand completions—is available on the popular YouVersion app.

Lindsey lives in Indianapolis, Indiana, with her husband and their three children. When she is not at home binge-watching *Schitt's Creek* or shuffling kids to their respective extracurricular activities, you'll most likely find her sipping wine with a friend, taking her dog Benny on a hike, or dropping her kayak in the water on those warm summer days.

Read more about Lindsey and get in touch with her online at www.LindseyFrazier.me.